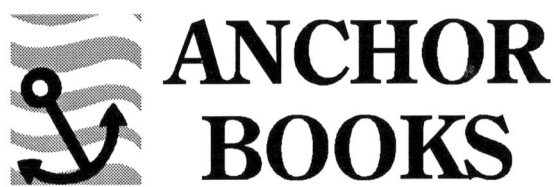

INSPIRATIONS 2002

Edited by

Heather Killingray

First published in Great Britain in 2002 by
ANCHOR BOOKS
Remus House,
Coltsfoot Drive,
Peterborough, PE2 9JX
Telephone (01733) 898102

All Rights Reserved

Copyright Contributors 2002

HB ISBN 1 85930 561 X
SB ISBN 1 85930 566 0

FOREWORD

For many of us the medium of poetry offers us a voice - a voice to speak out and let others know what we feel, think and desire. It is the vital bridge of communication that lets us share our innermost thoughts and messages on life to people who may need that vital surge of poetic inspiration.

Each of the chosen poems have been specifically favoured from a large selection of entries sent. As always, editing proved to be a difficult task and as the editor, the final selection was mine.

Inspirations 2002 is a unique collection of poetry and verse written in a variety of styles and themes, brought to us from many of today's modern and traditional writers, who reside in this area. The poems are easy to relate to and encouraging to read, offering engaging entertainment to their reader.

This delightful collection is sure to win your heart, making it a companion for life and perhaps even earning that favourite little spot upon your bookshelf.

Heather Killingray
Editor

Contents

Winter's Landscape	Moe Sherrard-Smith	1
A Sheltered Life	Caryn Saunders-Squires	2
Day Of Long	Marcus McNeill	3
Spring	Ivy Evans	4
Sweet Antonio	Lisa Burgess	5
The Cottage Of My Dreams	Kathleen Keech	6
Confidence	Nicola Grant	7
In The Spotlight	Kathryn West	8
The Renovation	Marcus Tyler	9
Peterborough Old Girls	Karen Davies	10
Animal, Vegetable, Mineral	David May	11
Number Two	W Smith	12
Spring Has Sprung	Barbara Goode	13
A Hot And Funny Day	Leanna Warrener	14
The Cup-Bearer	Kathleen O'Farrell	15
Simple Pleasures	Brian Thompson	16
Only One Penny	Mary McNulty	17
World Of Darkness	Cynthia Ann Cannon	18
Love	Andrew Crump	19
Elegy In A Lonely Churchyard	Susan Watson	20
Gentle Foal	Vivien Bailey	21
When Will Freedom Come?	Anon	22
Autumn Days Are Here Once More	Dawn Fox	23
Wanderer (Or A Definite Maybe)	B L Haswell	24
Real Or Imagined?	Lynn Jones	25
Goodnight . . . God Bless	Nicola Ransom	26
The Keeper Sleeping	Sharon Louise Martin	27
Today	Lisha Naomi Binns	28
The Bird Table	Faye Godfrey	29
Black Beauty	Alex Martin	30
Active Volcano	Katie F Munday	31
Chasing Trains	Simon Fairs	32
The Beauty At Night	Charles Hepburn	33
The Meaning Of Life	Kate Long	34
Once There	Dave White	35

Regrets	Margaret Meagher	36
Bed And Breakfast	Diane Berthelot	37
The Rose!	Brian Akers	38
Aspirations	Geoff Gaskill	39
Long Distance Love	B V Scotney	40
Drought	Glenys Gray	41
This Planet Of Strife	Robert Baslington	42
To My Dear Wife Marjorie	Bernard Wright	43
Prophet Of Doom	Jenny Bosworth	44
Eye Of The Storm	Paul Walton	45
Fight For A Civilised World	Jodie Bradshaw	46
Hibernation	Fred Smith	48
Outside With Bill	Keith L Powell	49
A Walk Along Southend Sea Front	Gwen Place	50
Mothers	Linda Finch	51
Getting Old	C Matthews	52
Remembering	John Jones	53
The River Remembers	Ron Hails	54
It Was Murder!	Ann Hutchison	55
The Scarecrow	P W Pidgeon	56
The March Of Time	Sheila B Fry	57
I'll Do It Later	Nicole Tomlin	58
Spring-In-All-Its-Glory	Audrey Williams	60
Technology	Chas Dainty	61
Another Land	V T Hardy	62
Ah Well!	Eunice Wightman	63
Lunacy	F Jones	64
Could I Be A Poet?	Stella Jones	65
Captain Webb's Peaceful Expansion	Peter Haines	66
My Childhood Wartime	Eddie Owers	68
Loneliness	Angie Garner	69
The Last Season	Ernest Brooks	70
Missing You	Lisa Bristow	71
Who!	Leonard Muscroft	72
SAD	Marion Evans	73
Give And Take	Sheila Hardwick	74

An Older Generation	J M Tyler	75
Earthbound	David Sewell Hawkins	76
The Passing Of The Nation's Favourite Grandmother	David Muncaster	77
Untitled	Frank Oldfield	78
Mud-Puddle Child	Trish Walton	80
North Yorkshire	J Ellison	81
A Touch Of Dutch	Rosemary Yvonne Vandeldt	82
Our Pat	Kathleen Hackleton	84
Sea Graves	Pauline M Parlour	85
Who Would Like A Toy Boy	Kathleen Wheeler	86
The Garden Of Love	Gillian Walsh	87
Life's Value?	John M Beazley	88
Time	Joan May Wills	89
The Truth	Dawn Graham	90
A Little Bird	Francis Allen	91
Starlight Wonder	Sheila E Harvey	92
The Air Held Change!	Peter James O'Rourke	93
A World Around Us	Roger Thornton	94
Cause Of Death	Clare Anne Lewis	95
Blue Glass On A Grey Day	Elizabeth Thorpe	96
My Son, My Love, Where Are You?	Mei Yuk Wong	97
A Day In The Sun	Brian Bates	98
Now It's For Real	Maggy Copeland	99
Demolition	Ann G Wallace	100
We Are What We Are	K W Benoy	102
The Gift	Katherine Parker	103
Words Of Love	Stella Bush-Payne	104
Uninvited Guest	Brenda Dove	105
Sweet Meadows	Maureen Margaret Huber	106
Deluge Of Death	Jane England	107
Wait Awhile	Ruth Kavanagh	108
Dream Of India	Elizabeth A Wilkinson	109
Jessie Ham	Alan Dawes	110
The Last Resting Place	G J Cayzer	112
Slow Down	Angela Pritchard	114
You Were . . .	Laura Nixon	115

Solitude And Tears	John Leighton	116
Still Hibernating?	Muriel Berry	117
My Valentine	Michael McNulty	118
Happy And Warm	S Glover	119
Mum	Sheryll Janet Hubbard	120
My Perfect Heaven	Jonty Holt	121
Stunned By It All	Florence Taylor	122
Anonymous II	Pauline Scragg	123
Just A Game	Martin Jordan	124
Where Lives A Prayer For You	David Bridgewater	125
Long Distance	Patricia Cunningham	126
Dyn Hybys	Alfa	128
Street Names In Formby Village	Freda Grieve	130
Faith	D H Taylor	131
How Lovely	Joan Smith	132
Cuerden Park	Robert Allen	134
The Mad Hatter	Margaret Hughes	135
My Mother	Caroline Ashton	136
New Baby	Matthew Ferguson	137
The Woman In The Photograph	James Ashworth	138
Within The Forest Of Pendle	David A Carter	139
Hope For The World	Anne E Marshall	140
Over The Moor	Trevor Howarth	141
Going Home	Olwyn Kershaw	142
She Of Heavens	Jason Redvers Latham	143
Incy Tipsy Spider	Hazel Ratcliffe	144
Full Circle	Hazel Wellings	145
The Hill Of Life	Olwena Reed	146
Jenny's Morning Poem	Paul Phelps	147
The Blue Tit	Margaret Pawson	148
Princess For A Day	B Page	149
Our Pendle	Doris Shire	150
Lifeline	Katherine Quaye	151
A Dream Just Before Wakening	Barry Jones	152
March Moon	Dione Burrow	153
My Favourite Things	Sheila Elkins	154
Hush Be Quiet!	B W Jones	155

Children Are Lent To Us, Not Given	Sally Hunter	156
An Avenue To Knowledge	M Yaqub Mirza	157
The Department Store After Sixty Years	Dora Hawkins	158
Noise	Mary Shepherd	159
Intimations Of Hope	Januarius	160
Questions!	Dev Dhaliwal	161
As I Looked Out Of The Window	M Carr	162
Farewell To Stan	Douglas Bryan Kennett	163
The Bluebell Wood	Bernard Laughton	164
Moonlight	Alistair L Lawrence	165
Thoughts In Drought	Christina Hanson	166
Estuary	Zardee Emmanuel Garagan	167
Football	D Stripling	168
The Angelus	Neilea Hames	169
Dogs	Nicole Jenkins	170
Weathers	Siobhan Jenkins	171

WINTER'S LANDSCAPE

Shelled round by its crystalline silence,
Earth sleeps, its malcontents buried
in picture postcard symmetry,
trapped by the hardness
pictures fail to urge upon the eye.

Time immemorial oaks, slumbering
sap-safe and tap-rooted,
stark against the whiteout of daybreak,
litter fields.

Slink whiskered stoat hungers flat
and quick nimbled on its urgent quest,
footfalls lingering
the crisp boundaries of exploration.
High above, the restless sheen of grey-white
marauds the emptiness, unsatisfied,
fluffs feathers against
the unaccustomed rhythm of the snow,
returns to familiar patterns
of blue-green seas.

While the carrion pickers,
sensible in age garnered wisdom,
quarter the salt-grit tarmac
for man-made litter and carnage
gloating, full stomached, homeward.

Earth sleeps, and here a full bud
tempts of spring.

Moe Sherrard-Smith

A Sheltered Life

He is there in the town centre
Sitting on a bench in the sheltered precinct,
There is no expression upon his face,
Void of memory, thoughts extinct.

His medication is administered
To dampen his irrationality,
And for times when paranoia is extreme
It helps to shelter him from reality.

He avoids all form of contact,
Denying love, thus sheltered from pain,
As he sits for another hour
To shelter from the rain.

When, at last, his labelled chore of sitting
Can be safely replaced upon the shelf,
He wanders back to his sheltered housing,
Where he can be safely sheltered from himself.

Caryn Saunders-Squires

DAY OF LONG

There's nothing like a summer's bloom
To raise you after nightly moon
To wondrous light and nature's call
And day of long, best of all.
The flowers seem to know the time
Displaying all their seasonal sign
And birds of song in wings of flight
Sing up to show their sheer delight
The carpeted floor with blossom fell
In garden of the wishing well
And times of beauty jump to thought
And an open mind I'm glad we caught
You notice things that once were blind
Your eyes get drawn by nature's kind
There's nothing like the summer's bloom
To raise you after nightly moon.
To wondrous light and nature's call
And day of long, best of all.

Marcus McNeill

SPRING

When winter snow has almost gone
And blackbirds burst into song
When I hear the first lambs bleating in the lane
And the sun shines warm through my windowpane
When the catkins from the branches dangle
And life seems good from every angle
When aconites lift up their heads and turn their faces to the sun
I know in my heart that spring has come.

Ivy Evans

SWEET ANTONIO

Soulmates strolling on silken sand lit by moonlight.
The coldness touches me,
Antonio notices and whispers,
His warm love forcing darkness to release its hold.

Words entered me with passion indescribable.
Precious sweet words he spoke,
Melting in through my soul, they filled my heart.
Our joining of spirit, a heavenly match.

He kissed me bittersweet of his Marlboro taste.
The almost rugged looks
To match his animal aroma and wild eyes,
Yet, eyes conveying his every ounce of love for me.

I could gaze upon his loving face forever.
Old eyes of jaded green,
And wisdom past his twenty-seven years.
A man of worldly strength with everything to give.

Sweet Antonio, so polite, so true, so kind.
Sensitive Antonio,
Who held me all night long, who cared for me,
More than any man I'd ever loved before.

Lisa Burgess

THE COTTAGE OF MY DREAMS

The cottage of my dreams,
Stands near a running stream,
With roses round the door,
And rush mats on the floor.

By the fire a black cat sits,
And Granny in her rocker, knits,
In the cottage of my dreams.

Through the window of my room,
I see flowers of abundance bloom,
And birds upon the treetop sing,
Church bells in the distance ring,
In the cottage of my dreams.

Kathleen Keech

CONFIDENCE

I notice the knocks,
the little dents to your self-esteem,
your cheeky smile and bright intelligence.
You want to shine,
But underneath it all,
You're afraid to fall,
in the estimation of others.
Act the clown, be the fool.
If you show indifference,
the mockery will miss the mark.
Your attitude stifles you,
the help half-hearted hindrance
further crushing your confidence.

Nicola Grant

IN THE SPOTLIGHT

The bright light falls in the evening sky,
I am snowed with a white spotlight.
Covered in magic, I have stars in my eyes.
The black pavement beneath me, my stage.
Powdered and ready, the show begins . . .

I rewind my mind and play the familiar music again.
The black shadows around me move, music notes gliding
Down the street, silhouettes of the past.

A flash of emerald eyes as a cat leaps the pavement, looks back.
A flashback of my youth, costumes decorated
With emerald sequins, reflected the stage lights.

I shone in the theatre's sphere.
Grass cries crystal tears,
Gentle glances of glistening glass
Glow in glimmers of moonlight.

Limping, I approach my home.
I hear my footsteps: a heavy step and the tap of my stick,
Shuffle, tap, shuffle, tap.
Remember those tap dancing routines?
Colourful tunes paint the pavement.

I hear a rustling and a heavy gust of wind,
My head bows and leaves collect at my feet.
The curtains draw, the applause dies.
The snow of light slowly melts and images blur.

Two trails of steam intertwine, like dancers,
Partners in unison.
I warm my hands, take a sip.
A step back, where the stage is my home.

Kathryn West

THE RENOVATION

People came from far and wide, to have a look - to see inside
The house they made as good as new, its popularity slowly grew.
The door was slammed over again, as they arrived in droves of ten
To watch the bricky build his wall, and the old one demolished and fall.
Three weeks of hell will soon be four, first of all they moved the door,
Now a window stands in place and of that door there is no trace,
They ripped out windows and put in new, replaced the bath,
sink and loo,
Ripped up floorboards rotten with worm, just the thought
makes me squirm.
The sparkie came and did his bit, a pretty nice job I must admit,
A chippy hung the exterior door, the rain seeps in and soaks the floor.
The living room is out of bounds, no longer can I watch
the postman's rounds,
The door won't shut it needs a shave, now the walls we have to save.
The kitchen stands stripped and stark, the appliances stand alone
in the dark,
We sit and watch the black and white in our bedroom every night,
As we sit in despair and wait, for the end, to celebrate,
For all the work in hand be done, this experience is not much fun.
Workmen stand round drinking cups of tea, discussing the state
of our economy,
Messing around with bits of wood and not doing the job they should.
We live in a bedroom all cramped in, until the structural engineer
has bin,
To have a look at the supporting beam, this is a nightmare
with a dream.
This experience I have to say, is a nightmare every day,
If you wish for a renovation, just read this poem of my frustration.

Marcus Tyler

PETERBOROUGH OLD GIRLS

To those who missed the reunion I say, shame on you, my friend.
What happened to your unbound loyalty? Why did you not attend?
Where is the moral fibre the teachers did their best to install,
Into fragile minds and hearts each morning in the assembly hall?

Not of the wilting variety, we girls of the County Grammar School.
Woe betide any man or woman, who tries to play us for a fool.
Timid and uncertain, we may have been on that very first day.
Certainly after five years, undesirable traits were sluiced away.

Strict regimes, codes of conduct, we did our best to embrace.
How does one wear gymslips and brown knickers with a sense
                                                        of grace?
Leotards for PE, thank heavens we were all girls.
Window cleaners received an eyeful when they came to call.

Hockey in sub zero temperatures, games mistress was one of a breed.
Offer a sick note? You were brave. No place for weakness in her creed.
It built strength of character, promoted the constitution of an ox.
What happened to sweet little girls in cotton poplin frocks?

The lady was actually there herself, on the above-mentioned occasion.
Still forthright in her manner, no change in her persuasion.
You've got fat, she said to me, as complimentary as ever.
You've got old, I should have said, but it's not in my nature, I'd never.

For myself, I met a friend, I'd not seen for twenty-seven years.
We hugged and laughed, felt inside the unmistakable sting of tears.
For time passed, and all that's happened between then and now,
                                                        it's strange,
How, to the influence of certain people, you attach a kind of blame.

Some faces, I recognised, photographs brought back happy memories.
A school steeped in tradition and high expectations, appropriate for me.
As we drank wine and reminisced of the pranks we used to pull,
In accord we all agreed, our schooldays were by no means dull.

Karen Davies

ANIMAL, VEGETABLE, MINERAL

You say that:
    As I do not hear it shout
    When I hook and land a trout,
    This does not mean that fishes feel no pain.
    You say I should not angle . . .
    Now my head is in a tangle
    With more concerns to exercise my brain.

You see:
    I do not hear a shout
    When I pick a Brussel sprout.
    Does this mean that brassica do not have feelings?
    Do I heed my need to feed
    Or renounce the heinous deed
    In the light of soundless vegetable squealings?

So then:
    Eat minerals you say,
    That's the only humane way.
    But are you sure that silicon won't suffer?
    Come on fella - get a life!
    There's no need for all this strife.
    Which one of us is just a silly duffer?

David May

NUMBER TWO

Two open blue eyes
Two lips so red
Two little ears.
One on each side of his head
Two darling wee feet
All these belong
To the baby so sweet.

W Smith

SPRING HAS SPRUNG

Eyes open so wide, you move off the step,
Looking around, know you've seen nothing yet.
Gone in and out, mind on what next you'll do.
Now's time to study magic all around you.

Spring's worked its spell by warming the air,
Earth's clumps have broken, instead brown soil lies there,
Up through the layers, green shoots pushing through,
gives a reminder, work on garden must do.

Weeds to be pulled, then in compost bin go.
Bushes to be shaped, loosen base soil with hoe.
Daffodils, snowdrops all showing bright heads,
Violet are spreading to form a blue ledge,

Fishpond needs cleaning, that job goes to Dad.
Grandpa assists him, the pair are so glad,
With this fine weather can spend time outdoors.
Enjoying the bounty of crisp green lawn floors.

Because it needs cutting give both extra work.
But doing their share, neither of them will shirk.
The children also enjoy having small jobs to do.
Collecting rubbish to put in dustbin bags too.

When we are together opinions are aired,
About our little Eden contentedly shared.
Picnic on green lawn, agree that the scene,
Result of our labour is fit for our Queen.

Barbara Goode

A Hot And Funny Day

I sat beneath a tree one day
on a hot and funny day.
Trying to remember what had been . . .
Had been . . .
Funny that day,
On that hot and funny day.

It took all the next day and
all the next night.
But even then I couldn't
remember what had been funny,
On that hot and funny day.

If you asked me I'd say I'd
had 'A hard day's night'.
But even now I still can't
remember what was funny.
On that hot and funny day.

Leanna Warrener

THE CUP-BEARER

He doesn't know, he'll never know,
For he'd be cross indeed,
If he learned that in my thoughts
I call him Ganymede . . .

So slim and straight and lithe he is,
And just on ten years old,
With dreamy eyes of velvet brown,
And hair of sleekest gold.

In Ancient Greece, I picture him
Beneath an olive tree,
Proffering nectar to the gods,
Upon a bended knee . . .

A gentle boy, a graceful boy,
Who served his masters well,
On Mount Olympus, when the world
Was young, as old books tell.

And now, I gaze upon this lad,
So like him, in his way,
But change will come, he won't remain
The child he is today . . .

A child, who bears a modern name,
Which suits him, I concede,
Yet, in my heart, will always be
My grandson - Ganymede!

Kathleen O'Farrell

SIMPLE PLEASURES

Try it. Try it.
Forget the diet.
Eat chocolate cake with dips.

Buy it. Buy it.
Go on and try it.
Eat sausage, egg and chips.

Fry it. Fry it.
Forget the diet.
Don't think about your hips.

Simple pleasures ...
or
... Sinful pleasures?

Brian Thompson

ONLY ONE PENNY

When is a Penny worth more than gold?
When Penny's your dog, and you've watched her grow old
She started our family, as a pup
And played with the kids as they grew up

She put up with many a playful tug
All made better with a loving hug
Sharing our lives, and giving us pleasure
So much fun and memories to treasure

She knew each day, when it was time to feed
And the excitement when she saw her lead
She knew the way we went for a walk
And the dogs we'd meet, when we stopped to talk

She meant everything to us, the perfect pet
But sometimes ill, and got help from a vet
No more suffering just a happy release
We know she'll be waiting, resting in peace

No more welcomes at the door
No more seeing her on the kitchen floor
Faithful and loyal right to the end
But one day we'll meet, and our hearts will mend.

Mary McNulty

WORLD OF DARKNESS

How I recall in days gone by
The sights I saw in God's blue sky
Soft white clouds sweeping across
As breezes blow . . .
Gently on my cheeks I feel the breeze,
Knowing that tall golden daffodils
Are swaying to and fro,
Birds in flight stopping here and there
Collecting bits and pieces
For their nests,
Alas . . . it was a lovely sight,
Droning planes winging their way to
Countries far beyond are but a memory
In my mind, now that I'm blind.
How glad I am I took the time to
Notice these wonders, before my world
Of darkness closed around me . . .
Thank God for days gone by.

Cynthia Ann Cannon

LOVE

What is love, is it enough?
Does it always seem so tough?
Is there a love that's perfect
Or does it always cause a profound effect?

Cuddles, hugs, a loving kiss.
Everyone deserves it, no one should miss.
A fluttering heart that needs a kick start.
There is a gap when we are apart.

Having a love that's so deep.
You feel it so, it's yours to keep.
Covering you in a loving shadow,
Far and wide, always big, never narrow.

Here to stay, don't go away.
Always real, not a make believe play.
Never quiet, a special delight.
I'm here to stay, I will never take flight.

A loving romantic cuddle.
Bodies entwined a lovers' muddle.
My love for you is so endearing,
You're great, a perfect mate, a bond never disappearing.
All the fun of a love we are sharing.

Andrew Crump

ELEGY IN A LONELY CHURCHYARD

Who were you?
The child in the churchyard
Whose stone I pass each time
I visit my father's grave.

Someone must have missed you once,
Have cried hopeless tears at your leaving.
Now you are at peace, but long forgotten.
No one speaks your name anymore.
Am I the only one who looks now?
Am I the only one who places flowers
On your resting place?
I must be.

All you knew have followed you,
Passed away, resting,
Their bones now dust again.
Why you call me and touch my heart
I don't know.
I only know I cannot pass your tiny grave.
Its small stone cross embossed in lichen
Upon which is inscribed:
Katherine Kirk,
Departed this life
May 17th 1902
Aged 4 years.
Another angel for Heaven.

Susan Watson

GENTLE FOAL

Gentle foal born of your mother
Morning sun shines down on you.
Gazing around, a world is given
Life begins, as dreams unfold.

Misty eyes just breaks my heart
Wishing I cold take you home.
But I know, that I could not
I shall leave you there to roam.

Melt me with your gentle whining
Caress you there, one hundred fold.
Till your eyes begin to flicker
Dream on now, till the break of dawn.

Vivien Bailey

WHEN WILL FREEDOM COME?

When will freedom
Take me home,
To the valleys
Where I shall roam?

When will freedom
Set me free,
Return me to
My family?

When will freedom
Spread her wings,
Carry me home
On western winds?

When will freedom
Break my chains,
So I can walk
Summer's country lanes?

When will freedom
Let me go
To the people
I love and know?

Anon

AUTUMN DAYS ARE HERE ONCE MORE

Autumn days are here once more,
Icy winds and misty mornings,
The forecast says we're in for another downpour.

Hallowe'en comes with witches, bats,
A spooky tale to tell,
To give us a fright,
Trick or treat is what we hear on that night.

Next it's rockets, bangers and the sky is full
Of bright light,
Then you know it's Guy Fawkes night.

The trees are stripped of their foliage,
Left naked and bare,
The wildlife forage for the berries,
Seeking out anything that might be still there.

Green, yellow, red, gold and brown,
The colours of the leaves that fall.

The days draw to an early close,
Daylight fades, cold nights come to chill us all.

So shut the curtains,
Turn the heat on,
Snuggle up close together,
Until you hear the birds' song.

Dawn Fox

WANDERER (OR A DEFINITE MAYBE)

But you swim in different ways,
What are we to think?
I'd almost made my mind up.
Well, perhaps, on the brink.

Ask me if I am schizophrenic,
I answer, er, yes and no.
Imagination runs riot, daydreams soar.
Life's intuition, that I know.

But then, you see, I'm psychic.
I love the purple and blue.
Reality has no meaning for me.
Facts do not resemble the true,

Wildly wander, meaningless meander,
Back spiral of life's path.
Tell, do you know who you are?
Yes, Piscean, um, I think I am.

Reader, you travel life's zodiac.
What is it that you feel?
Pisces can read you inside out.
You must stay on the wheel!

To emerge in one's true colours,
Deception is a shameful sham.
Pisceans are sharp as all the rest.
I believe. Therefore, I am!

Such a self defence mechanism.
Beyond conception of military mind.
Pisceans are not what they openly portray.
Dig into them, and what will you find?

B L Haswell

REAL OR IMAGINED?

They're out there you know
They really exist
In silvery moonlight
And pearly dawn mist

They're there in the glare
Of the midday sun
From twilight to starlight
Till day is done

I've seen them through showers
Watching them dance
Leap-frogging flowers
Round buttercups prance

Out in the meadow they'll gaily play
Hiding and seeking amongst the hay
Running through cornfields, cowslip and heather
Lilly-pad hopping down at the river
Climbing and sliding down slippery reeds
Feasting on daisy and dandelion leaves

And here and there in shaded dells
Swinging from stems of sweet bluebells
You'll hear their voices soft and low
On gentle breezes to and fro

Will o the wisps, Jack Frost and imps
Fairies, goblins and elves I have glimpsed
Wood nymphs and pixies, winged angels too
Have been my companions my whole life through
And real or imagined I must insist
You know they're out there
They really exist.

Lynn Jones

GOODNIGHT . . . GOD BLESS

If you are looking down from above,
Send to me your protection and love,
Listen to this prayer that I say,
And save my soul for one more day.

May your angels guard me as I sleep this night,
Singing their sweet song 'til the morning light,
And please keep from evil all those who I hold dear,
Let seraphic images defend them from fear.

Give me the strength to cope with another tomorrow,
Deliver me the courage to live through the sorrow,
Steer me from the path of darkness, temptation and sin,
Make me deaf and blind to the devil, let my love win.

When my time is nigh may my soul to Heaven you take,
Please forgive me my sins as my body I forsake,
Hallow me if you will your eternal Heavenly host,
In the name of the Father, the Son and the Holy Ghost . . .
Amen.

Nicola Ransom

THE KEEPER SLEEPING

The light from my heart is with you,
The peace from me surrounds you,
Go as you will, but heed my warnings of love's lost heart.

Dream of summer days, lush fields, corn bobbing,
Skies never ending, like my love for you, eternal, glowing.
Aspire to the heights, run to the edge, do not fear,
I am here to catch you falling.

The change may hurt my love, no doubt it will, but
Swallow as a bitter pill - no gain without pain, 'tis true enough.

But oh, what joy to behold, when you emerge, bold
And bright as a sunbeam, fresh from Heaven's rays
To run and fall and laugh amongst the fields.
The yellow gold which now you hold within your soul.

Awakened by the touch of light, no more to dwell
In darkened pastures, your mind, your soul, your body,
Full of love and rapture.
Never in this life shall its door be closed;
For once returned to your home pure and true,
Life holds only beauty for you.
The keeper of your own happiness and heart's desire.

Sharon Louise Martin

TODAY

Today of all days was a good day
A good memory, which would never pass.

Who could ever image the amount of excitement,
Which could happen in one day
One day
One single day
One whole day

And the reason it was a good day
Was it couldn't of happened on a better day

What joy has passed but will indefinitely grow
Grow as old as me
And die with me

That's how I know today was a good day.

Lisha Naomi Binns

THE BIRD TABLE

I'm standing here watching the birds on the table,
Taking away as much as they're able.
I put seeds and breadcrumbs out there for the feast.
The starlings are greedy, I like them the least.
The finches are robins fly in from above,
Every so often there's a soft cooing dove.
There's squabbling and shrieking and feathers a-flutter,
A gull's got a whole slice of bread, with some butter!
When the ground is so hard with winter's cold frost
A fine meal of earthworms to these birds is lost.
So I'll hang out the fat balls and cut rind off the bacon.
Perhaps then these small creatures will not feel forsaken.

Faye Godfrey

BLACK BEAUTY

I have a cat
And she ain't fat.

She's sleek and streamline,
Some people call her feline.

She has eyes from Neptune
And claws, that have touched the moon.

She licks her tail all the time,
And loves tinned fish in oil or brine

She dips her paws in the pond,
She'd find it easier if she had a wand.

So that's my cat,
She's as good as an aristocrat.
Or, is that aristocat?

Alex Martin

ACTIVE VOLCANO

The volcano old, yet so bold
Sizzling and roaring, the volcano is pouring
Rising and leaping, showering and deepening
In its rocky cave below
Its moaning and groaning and shaking and quaking
A man's voice shouts, 'Get out, get out'
It's starting to roar, it's going to pour
It's rattling and battling,

The lava is blistering
Flaming and bubbling, nothing can stop it doubling
Swirling and toiling, scorching and boiling
Down it flows to the valley below
Sizzling and whizzing, hissing and fizzing
Destroying everything in its course by its mighty force
Nothing is safe of its wrath
It's daring and uncaring,

The volcano not so red now it's dead
Grey and quiet, no more riot
Gas and air, rancid and rare
The molten rock is cooling
Silent and still, lifeless and tranquil
No more ash coming down, changing the shape of the town
It's now calm, no more harm
The volcano stops raging but continues ageing.

Katie F Munday (9)

CHASING TRAINS

I sit here counting many trains,
Passing me by in the rain, wanting for you.
Living my days by a train timetable,
Empty from you, couldn't you call, weren't you able?
Or maybe you're not thinking of me.

I've looked in all the other cars,
Checked empty trains and station bars,
A glimpse for what I hoped to see.
But now I sit here at a café table,
Cigarette in hand and a friend in a bottle,
Just a Stella Artois and me,

So won't you take a little time out for today?
Put a smile on my face with your presence with me,
By taking your place by my side in these hard times,
'Cause I really want you and if you really want me,
We can now forever be.

I've never been one for killing time,
But from sun up to sundown I'd shine, only for you.
The times we'd speak on the telephone,
Planning our love and our very own,
Meetings that would never be.

I feel my heart's let slowly down,
Built back up then spun around, searching for you.
Now my train's stopped and I've got off,
At an unmanned station free of cost,
For all lonely hearts and me.

So won't you take a little time out for today,
Put a smile on my face with your presence with me.
By taking your place by my side in these hard times,
'Cause I really want you and if you really want me,
We can now forever be.

Simon Fairs

THE BEAUTY AT NIGHT

I hear love softly singing to me in angelic harmony
Each chance I have to sing of your love
Like fields of red roses, you reap the love
My heart has sown for you.

Love's mystic hand has touched my heart
As my heart beats out in patterns of love
Flowers bloom at her feet as I listen in silence
To your voice so sweet.

Your eyes glow with passion as I look into
Your eyes like cool still waters in beautiful shades
Of blue as I dance in your eyes of beauty.

The gentle caress of your soft words with
Your golden hair that swirls like wind blown
Wisps of mists that move to the motions of love.
I held her love in my hand for infinity

My dreams arise from behind my eyes as I sing
To the stars of the love of my dreams and in the
Mornings I weep for the love of you.

As the emotions of passion a loving embrace
Your kisses gentle like soft virgin snowflakes
Placed upon my lips,
Your skin your smile your beautiful face, for you
Are the beauty I see at night as my love belongs
To you.

Charles Hepburn

THE MEANING OF LIFE

Who knows what they really want in life?
Is it the only life?
We can only guess and follow our dreams,
Our hearts.
Dreams can be so powerful, but what do they mean?
What does anything mean in this journey we call life?
How do we control what goes on in life?
The one simple answer is
Love.
We will always be in love, you and I,
But what love I don't know. I will never know.
I hope one day you will make friends with this wonderful feeling,
This four lettered word which means so much in our hearts.
I have made friends a long time ago.
You will choose the right path one day,
But not mine,
Because my path has been taken
By this little friend I have come to know.

Kate Long

ONCE THERE!

My life has taken yet another turn
    within a twist for the worst.
Am I really that wicked,
        to be souly cursed.
Or has my sense of perception
Simply fallen prey
        to an artful deception?

Divorce looks to be inevitable,
But is it to be, really regrettable,
Or just blatantly unforgettable.
Four children are involved.
With their teenage life to be
        as yet unsolved?
And our youngest child's
Just psychologically effected but
        not yet wild!
It's like a game of charades
Inside a shadow of guess what's
        happening,
Behind only what the shadow's knowing.
I'm feeling, much as an antelope
Out upon a mountainous slope
    Wishing only for to graze;
But nothing's there:
Whilst inwardly I mystically gaze
    Although outwardly I steer;
Captivated by the sheer memory
        Of what was once there!

Dave White

REGRETS

In every life regrets form a large crowd
Angry words so quickly and rashly spoken
But to admit we were wrong we were too proud
In moments a precious friendship is forever broken

Words of love that we never got to say
Afraid to reach out and make our feelings clear
Alas now has passed the opportunity and the day
Failure to be willing to make a commitment can cost us dear

Wrapped up in our own busy and frantic life
We do not heed our loved one's desperate cry
Do not see that their life is full of trouble and strife
To take the time to comfort them we do not try

So many moments lost and gone for ever more
Opportunities that were never seized and taken
Pride or fear of failure made us reject the open door
But late in life those sleeping regrets will awaken

Regrets make for a sad and lonely old age
Never let the moment pass, tomorrow may be too late
Imprint your caring and love on every new page
You do not know what time is left, so do not wait

Better to have tried and failed, to love and lose
Than to end up regretful for not having tried
Every chance in life is there to seize and use
And hope that this time luck is on your side

Regrets are a sad epitaph, so make them few
Try to be positive, live a life that is full and caring
If you want to say something kind, give praise that is due
Make sure that in the end it is love, not regrets, you are sharing

Margaret Meagher

BED AND BREAKFAST

The blackbird turned to his 'partner' and said,
I know just the place to build our nest,
The Berthelots at No 2,
Have a thick, high hedge secured from view,
Mr 'B' bakes cakes, you see,
So plenty of titbits for you and me.
The only snag is 'Cleo' the cat,
Who wanders round for the occasional snack.
This family have all 'mod cons',
A birdbath and a garden pond,
So we can shower, eat and drink,
In other words live in the 'pink'.
I'll show you their garden tomorrow, my dear,
I feel in my 'feathers' it will be a good year,
And when our little ones come along,
We'll treat them all to a *full* bird song.

Diane Berthelot

THE ROSE!

There's nothing lovelier than the rose,
That beautiful scent
Beneath our nose!
The colour red is surely mine,
Outstanding like a godly shrine,
I love its shape its every curve,
Sometimes it's more than I deserve!
So if I'm tempted and not too kind,
I picture the rose within my mind,
Its beauty is beyond compare,
I can see it now suspended there,
So just find time and feel its presence!
God is there it's very essence!

Brian Akers

ASPIRATIONS

A nod and a wink.
A shrug, an arched eyebrow,
A half-spoken thought,
A planting of seed -
Said with a nuance,
A half-smile of sadness;
A soupcon of malice
Digesting the greed.

Stunned disbelief.
Faith starts to crumble.
Acquaintances shuffle.
Belligerence claws.
Treacherous glances.
Frozen expressions.
Sense of destruction
Without a *because*.

Tread softly; speak gently;
Deal well with each other.
Prepare in the open;
Conclude in the light.
Anything other
Friend, foe or brother
Could loose what you have;
Could put trust to flight.

Beware, O beware
As much as you can
That hateful destructor -
The tongue of a man.

Geoff Gaskill

LONG DISTANCE LOVE

My life consists of waiting,
For the phone, for a message
From my love
So many miles away.

Why do I do it?
Why not get on with my life
And forget him, and my dreams?
Because I cannot, I cannot.

He is in my heart and soul
In every fibre of my being.
He is everything I want
But cannot have.

I love him so much
I love to hear his voice
And to make him laugh
It makes me very happy.

Will we ever be together?
I don't think so.
I can only dream
Of what might have been.

All I know with certainty
Is that while I have breath
In my body
I will love him.

B V Scotney

DROUGHT

The parched ochre land
lies like a sunset
on the cracked earth.
Raw gaping wounds, bleed
dust to coat the trees.
Once a river flowed
where now crazy paving
creaks and moans as it limps
to the unforgiving sea.
Soulless eyes gaze skyward.
A million prayers reach out.
Not yesterday, not last year.
No rain has fallen.
And tears run dry.

Glenys Gray

THIS PLANET OF STRIFE

This planet is smitten with terrorism and strife,
With suicide bombers taking an innocent life.
To them their belief is to paradise they will go,
But a merciful God's answer will be no,

But this strife is caused by the different Religions' creed
For peace loving people it makes their hearts bleed.
So with bigotry and hate it will be hard to solve,
If only this could be forgiven peace may evolve.

But terrorists filled with venom and hate
If we can't find a compromise it may be too late.
Islamic hard liners wanting a holy war,
If they ignore God's teachings it will close the door.

The one God is the Omniscient Presence,
Unity to one God is of the essence.
The Christian teachings say you will not kill one another,
Because from God's creation we are sister and brother.

From thousands of years since our creation
Coming from the same source we must be a distant relation,
It was only the one God that created us from the primeval sod.
This indicates that we were created by the one God.

Robert Baslington

TO MY DEAR WIFE MARJORIE

Oh, Darling, how I miss you
On every single day.
After four and fifty years of marriage
What else could I say?
We lived our life in perfect bliss
Devoted to each other,
But now I am an empty shell
Devoid of nuptial cover.
But somewhere beyond man's vision,
In the great unknown,
I believe that you are waiting
So I'll no longer be alone.
One day we'll be together,
United for evermore,
To live again in happiness
On God's eternal shore.

Bernard Wright

PROPHET OF DOOM

I'm a prophet of doom
I always think the worst.
If there is a problem
I've thought of it first

People say why don't you change
Think the best, sing another tune.
But I'm a prophet of doom
And bad things will happen soon

Jenny Bosworth

EYE OF THE STORM

I was born in a place,
With no identity, no face,

In the eye of the storm,
Is where I was born,

In a world of friction,
No hope, no joy, only conviction,

In a world of hostility,
Death is a possibility,

I'd like to confess,
And put this to rest,

This world I'll be torn,
Is the eye of the storm.

Paul Walton

FIGHT FOR A CIVILISED WORLD

How can we go on now?
We cannot change the past.
The crime has been committed,
An impact made to last.
The victims' lives have perished;
They cannot be regained.
But why is it the blameless,
That have to feel the pain?
So many feelings build up:
Fear, anger, dread.
Hatred for the villains,
Sorrow for the dead.
From birth children are lectured
That violence should be condemned.
So why is it that adults
Are hating their fellow men?
For every man crowned a hero,
A thousand men have died.
In war there are no winners,
No prize for sacrificing pride.
Courage is forced upon those
Who stand up for what is best.
A reward for the fate of surviving?
An empty medal on the chest.
A day of tragedy has fallen upon us,
A nightmare in the mind.
Just like the battles and injustices
That will always plague mankind.
But that which does not kill us
Can only make us stronger,
And add to the links of unity,
To make the chain grow longer.

You can knock us down with force,
And break this fragile bond.
But we know we can grow back again
With hope; new-found and strong.
And stormclouds might just gather,
And raindrops might just fall,
But the sun will rise tomorrow,
And shine; shine for us all.

Jodie Bradshaw

HIBERNATION

As a grizzly bear I hibernate
Now that winter's here,
Tucked up in my cosy lair
There's nought for me to fear,
Unless of course there's another bear
Wants to share it too,
But such conduct's extremely rare -
In fact, in bearland it's taboo.
It would be regarded as a scandal
Though I wouldn't come off worse,
If I really had to share with him,
I'd make sure that he slept first.

Fred Smith

OUTSIDE WITH BILL

You're playing outside with Bill again
What is that laughter it does not sound the same
For it is loud there is no mistake
Just look at the garden now.

You're playing outside with Bill again
Really really it is starting to rain
You have changed the soil into mud
And killed all the flowers with my soap suds.

You're playing outside with Bill again
Just go and play away from here
Somewhere where it will not cost me dear
But have a happy time.

Keith L Powell

A WALK ALONG SOUTHEND SEA FRONT

The cliffs are ablaze with daffodils
Like yellow chiffon scarves,
They float and drift with gentle ease
Swaying 'neath the budding trees,
And oh the sun, the glorious sun
Lights them from within,
While early risen velvet bees
In and out them spin.

Transferring one's gaze to the other side
The view is maritime,
For silver dipped blue rippling waves
Dance in time to their own sea 'raves',
And still the sun, the glorious sun
Gives sparkle to their spray,
Yes it is close to Heaven on Earth
To be out on such a day.

Gwen Place

MOTHERS

Mothers are made up from a lot of things.
Firstly love, followed by kindness.
They are there at your first breath into this big world.
They are there when you are toddling about, and
Pulling things from your cupboards.
They help you when you hurt or graze yourself.
They are there when you start school for the very first time.
They give lots of encouragement and help you with your homework.
They are always there when you are sick or in pain.
They are there for the bad things of life.
They are there when you take that step up the aisle.
They are there when you bring her grandchildren into the world.
So when those arms and legs are tired, and those eyes are closing.
It's time to help them, and to give them love in return
For all the love and help they have given you.

Linda Finch

GETTING OLD

You think you're getting old
When your shoes are nearly flat
Not like the high stilettos
Yes you remember that

You think you're getting old
When you wear a thermal vest
Not like the pretty camisole
You once wore on your chest

You think you're getting old
When rose water you're a fan
You spray yourself daily
And smell just like your nan

You think you're getting old
When the chicks have flown the nest
It's time to do the things you planned
But all you do is rest

You know you're getting old
When in the glass you see
A wrinkled face staring back
Where your face used to be

You think you're getting old
Till one day when you're in pain
They play Elvis on the radio
And you're sixteen again

C Matthews

REMEMBERING

When I was young
And wrapped in the fire of a blazing sun
I ran in the painless flames of my blood
Ran
As life volcanoed in my easy brain
To drain
Down
Down
Through the warm moist dark of my supple veins
Living had just begun then
When I was young
And wrapped in the fire of a blazing sun

The days of my life slipped by
And so
I came to recognise an older age
With the unstoppable clock ticking on
Time had dulled the flames in my blood
And toughened those once such supple veins
But the memories have remained
And so
I nod and smile on that boy
That natural boy
Young
Ever young
And wrapped in the fire of a blazing sun

John Jones

THE RIVER REMEMBERS

Night softly falls as, wraith like, the mist probes to fill
the Essex Marshland, stealing along creek and over mossy banks.
In the cultured reaches, houseboats and pleasure craft
lie in lapping idleness by banks and shore;
and willows hang long arms to water's coolness.
Freshening tides, near the estuary, ring cautioning bells
from buoys marking the channels and blinking their warning
to shipping.

Now the Numen of the Thames arouses from slumber.
Memories stir, confused and muddled in times' repetitions
against the grey murk of marsh and dance of fireflies;
fractured moonglow glints on horned helmet and curving long boat;
Nordic tongues echo strangeness and menace in the blanketing mist,
lost in a welter of human grunts, drifting coracles
and sounds of foraging animals.
Floating on the air come cries of revelling and ravish from
riverside campfires, while, to the south are distant shrieks and moans
where 60,000 lock in hackings of mutual slaughter.
These fade, replaced by the rhythm of marching legions
and shouted orders.
Across the marshes the shadows pass of bearers
laying to rest the numberless victims of London's Plague.
Explosions rend the Docklands to the drone of aircraft and
popping ground fire:
Raging fires merge with those in the wake of Plague.
From gilded river craft music issues, mixing oddly
with thuds of dismembering from The Tower.
In a strange, greenish light of thinning mist
full-masted schooners ghost lazily with the tide,
and, in their wake, the outlines of high-decked, funnelled craft
and the 'toots' of awakening reality . . .
. . . To flooding light the curtain lifts,
And the River's Guardian fades from the night-time vigil.

Ron Hails

IT WAS MURDER!

It wasn't the fact that he gambled, m'lud,
Or the 'young bit' he had on the side.

It wasn't the fact that he beat me, m'lud,
Although that I just couldn't abide.

It wasn't the fact that he drank, m'lud,
No, the one thing I had to abhor,

Was the minute his head hit the pillow, m'lud,
He immediately started to snore!

Ann Hutchison

THE SCARECROW

Black eyeless sockets ever stare
Across the early planted field,
The guardian of seeds stands there,
An awesome sight.

With tattered jacket flapping wide
And o'er the wizen face a hat,
While arms of wood stretch either side
With grim intent.

Though the days both foul and fair
Still, this effigy of man
To fright the robber of the air,
Black-coated Thief.

The gaping mouth, the yellow lips
Throws his voiceless challenge out,
Whilst on his wide straight shoulder sits
The wiser crow.

P W Pidgeon

THE MARCH OF TIME

When you look in the mirror who do you see
Is it the girl you used to be
You may have got much older, and even changed your name
But beneath the lines and wrinkles, you will always be the same

The number on your birthday cards gets higher every year
But then it's only a number you say to those who want to hear
You don't feel any different from all those years ago
Perhaps a little stiffer and walk a little slow

The world is full of people who rush about and rage
Then turn around and tell us how we should act our age
It's don't eat this and don't eat that
You know it will only go to fat

You like to go out shopping and choose your clothes with care
No need to be told what you should and shouldn't wear
If you want to wear trousers then go ahead and strut your stuff
After all let's face it, the men have worn them long enough

Underneath your head of grey you don't have to try
Been there done that is your battle cry
They say everyone's living longer, but no one knows quite why
Could it be that though everyone wants to go to Heaven
No one wants to die.

Sheila B Fry

I'LL DO IT LATER

I've got my chocolate biscuits and I've made my millionth cup of tea.
At last I'm ready to do some work.
Ummm . . . I wonder if anyone ate that last toffee?

Getting down to do some work, isn't it the hardest thing to do?
Everything seems so much more exciting,
like doing the ironing, watching 'Neighbours', even cleaning the loo.
Right! I have plenty of time and I know it's got to be done!
It's no use, I'm not in the mood, I want to be out having fun!

As usual the time flies past, nothing seems to alter.
I start the day with great intentions
and end up dreaming of my holiday in Gibraltar.

OK! I'll have my lunch, then I will definitely get crackin'!
But then I need to watch that video.
Yes! I admit, it's will power I'm lackin'!

That's it! I've wasted enough time,
I have to do some work . . . after I've given a friend a call.
I don't believe it, it's happened again!
I've wasted another day doing sod all!

Hooray! I did it! I am so chuffed with myself,
I actually managed to make a start.
All right, so I only spent 20 minutes on my work,
But I still think I deserve that jam tart.

Oh no, my once, 'Plenty of time to get it done.'
Has practically run out.
If I don't knuckle down and burn that midnight oil.
I'll certainly be up the spout.

Oh why don't I ever learn to get things done straight away?
In fact next time I will ignore my 101 excuses,
and I won't leave things to the last minute . . .
Yeah, that will be the day!

Nicole Tomlin

SPRING-IN-ALL-ITS-GLORY

'Blossoms on the trees again
red, pink, white and yellow
loom proud across landscapes far and wide
giant bouquets in bloom amidst the countryside,
birds in flight singing on the breeze
collecting twigs and down as nesting time begins.
Grass a healthy green fresh from morning dew,
a multitude of colour with bulbs and flowers in bloom.
Soft white clouds float in pale blue skies
sprinkling showers refreshing light and few.
I saw a squirrel yesterday awake from winter sleep
rabbits, fieldmice, creatures many
emerge and take a peek.
Spring in all its glory how breathtakingly unique.'

Audrey Williams

TECHNOLOGY

We have the technology, learn'ed men say
Technology yesterday, tomorrow, today.
Have it for peace, have it for war
You can have it for a whole lot more.

It could be good, it could be bad
Some may say it's even mad.
It's here to stay you can be sure
For high and low, for rich and poor.

'What is technology?' you may ask
I tell you this, it's no easy task.
What would the world be if there were none?
The things we know would all be gone.

TVs, radios, cars and such
Of other things there would not be much.
Praise it, condemn it, whatever you may
You cannot escape it, it's here to stay.

This thing called technology!

Chas Dainty

ANOTHER LAND

Above the clouds is another land,
Where people walk hand in hand,
People reunited together again,
Never to be parted, and free from pain.
No evil, badness or hate,
Will ever get past this Heavenly gate.
In this land the people are the best,
Taken there for a well earned rest,
Everyone's happy, children play with glee,
Birds are always singing, and dogs run free,
It's a peaceful place where the sun shines bright
And silvery stars twinkle at night,
The ones we love are in this land,
And when it's time they will take our hand,
Leading us through the golden gate,
To a magical world, where there's no hate.

V T Hardy

AH WELL!

I'm not yet in my autumn years,
  But summer is definitely going
If only I could return,
  And in my past be knowing
The right and wrongs of what to do
  And how and when to do it,
Instead of sitting here and saying
  - I reckon I just blew it!

Eunice Wightman

LUNACY

'Listen!' The wavering fool
Exhorts the moon:
'You are too big and you
Have swelled too soon.'

The moon replies:
'You've slept too long the night,
Not watched my dimness turn to light,
Bright light, which might delight the sight,
Dispelling blighted night.'
The moon exhorts the lunatic: 'It's cool
To call at me, and dance across my pool
Of scattered radiance on the rain-swept ground.
I'm still around
To answer back, oh fool!'

The fool cries, with a great shout:
'I'll blot you out,
You and your light!
Here comes a gruesome cloud,
Thick, grey and purple. Now, however loud
You shout to me, I shall not hear,
I fear!
Moon! You and your lunar light!
Goodnight!'

F Jones

COULD I BE A POET?

When in the local paper, you did invite,
Poets to send in the things they write,
I thought that I would take the hint,
I have always wanted to appear in print.

Should I write about my life?
Mostly spent as a mother and wife,
Or my daughters, one, two, three
(They would not be pleased with me!)
Grandchildren, a girl and three boys,
(I cannot believe what I've spent on toys!)
The eldest now full grown,
Has children of his own,
Two are teenagers, adulthood coming fast,
My granddaughter, not least but last,
In September starts at Senior school,
When she speaks, everything is 'cool'
My neighbours where I live,
Who to all their friendship give,
People that I've known for years
That could only end in tears!
My garden, now so full of flowers,
After it rained for hours and hours.
Holidays I've spent abroad,
That no longer I can afford
The theatre, bingo, eating out,
What can I write about?

Nothing comes to mind,
Inspiration I cannot find,
So pen and paper I'll put away
Could I be a poet? Maybe someday!

Stella Jones

CAPTAIN WEBB'S PEACEFUL EXPANSION
(24/25 August 1875)

'Neath the chalk towers incessantly shrieking,
White wingéd hunters are swooping and seeking;
Gracefully flighting - on smooth waves alighting,
Splashing and dashing - a flurry of fighting.
Men looking seaward these antics are heeding
Awaiting the moment when they'll be leading
From harbour-haven to white water heaving
A mortal who will, the safe shore be leaving.

A warm August sun was westwardly dipping,
From the pier to the waves a figure was slipping;
Three leagues to France in the path of the gull,
But add two leagues more for the zigzagging hull
Of the wind-battered lugger cresting the foam
En-route to Calais from Dover her home -
With a swimmer not given a ghost of a chance
Of breasting the maelstrom from England to France.

Victoria reigned, scarlet spread far and wide,
But no army could help naked flesh against tide.
The might of the Empire with cannon and lance
Could not push this Briton one yard nearer France.
For the glory of England, but no fifes or drums,
Just trust in the pilot's tide-tables and sums.
Unlike his armed brethren on their glory trail
There'd be no reinforcements should he look to fail.

Dark wave met black cloud 'neath night's cold embrace,
The salt-wounded warrior was slackening pace -
Enmeshed in weed-mass 'gainst an alien tide -
But so far every obstacle had been defied
By this Shropshire sea-captain with a will of iron
Equal to any campaign-medalled 'lion'.
As his scarlet-clad brethren, the Empire expanded,
This lone unarmed battler on Calais' shore landed.

Peter Haines

MY CHILDHOOD WARTIME

I remember the day Neville Chamberlain gave us the news
It gave my mum, dad and me the blues -
We sat round the wireless to hear what he had to say
He said war had been declared on that Sunday -
The sirens sounded and there was still everywhere
To think what was ahead of us we did not dare -
We put up the blackout and checked our gas masks
My mum was busy with so many tasks -
Dad went as usual to work although it was hard
When he got home there was a letter from the Home Guard -
The letter he got had OHMS on and gave Mum a fright
She thought Dad has been called up and would have to fight -
I went to school with my gas mask in a box
Mum gave me dripping sandwiches and I had holes in my socks -
Our school was bombed and the ceilings came down
There was terrible damage all over the town -
Croydon aerodrome had planes that went up to fight
They even chased Germans from the sky at night -
We had Anderson shelters that were put in the ground
As you slept on the bunks you could hear every sound -
Ration books, identity cards and things in short supply
The Germans were relentless with their bombs from the sky -
Sticky tape was put on the windows just in case
Hitler dropped one of his bombs and blew glass in our face -
Stirrup pumps, water buckets and sandbags were at the front door
Walking down our street you could see everyone was at war.

Eddie Owers

LONELINESS

I awake with reluctance, outside birds are singing, the sun is shining, a new day is here.
But my heart feels heavy, my body cold with fear;
And despite tightly closed eyes, down my cheek rolls a tear.

With leaden feet I enter the kitchen, put on the kettle for a cup of good cheer;
Boil an egg, lay the table for one, then pull up a chair.
In minutes the house is tidied, the bed neatly made, it's far too big now there's no one to share.

Then it's off to the shops to buy food for one, but from where?
And on to the park where I sit and watch the children play, for as long as I dare.
Back home in the garden I pull up the weeds, which once were so rare;
You knew all about gardens and had 'green fingers' m'dear.

The evening meal over, at the TV I stare;
We used to play scrabble, talk over the day's events, but that's not possible now you're no longer here.
To fill in the crossword is no longer fun, no more your slippers warming by the hearth, the grate is redundant and bare.

You must get out and meet people friends loudly declare.
But when I ask to join them they shrug their shoulders and walk away in despair.
You see society is geared to couples so beware.

Nervously I check that all doors are secure, windows tight shut,
night burglars to deter, there's no one else to care.
Another day over, depressed and weary I kneel in prayer.
But as I lay counting sheep, dreading yet another nightmare,
A warm glow spreads over me because deep in my heart I know Christ Jesus is near.

Angie Garner

THE LAST SEASON

The fields are ready for the autumn plough
And the wind, has a bit more bite
Oh! How fast the seasons change
Almost, overnight
The birds are growing thick, their down
The horse's hair, grows long
No more across the open field
Can you hear the cuckoo song
The lambing days, have long gone by
They have delivered their last birth
The leaves are falling off the trees
And carpeting, the earth
Then as the winds get colder
They will bring with them the snow
To transform the countryside
With holly, and mistletoe
The children will be out to play
With sleigh and snowball fight
Their laughter will ring through the air
To add to the wondrous sight
With sleigh bells, and Father Christmas
Spreading peace, and all his joy
there will be smiles of glee, upon the face
Of every girl and boy
It's the time, that we call Christmas
A time, we cherish dear
For it's not only the last season
But the end, of another year.

Ernest Brooks

MISSING YOU

Upon the hill I sit and wait
But the sun goes to sleep
It is getting quite late
My heart is aching, tired and weak
A gentle tear rolls down my cheek
Still upon the hill I wait some more
For the angel I have grown to adore

I hear my name upon the breeze
Or is it the breeze as she plays with the trees?
An angel came to sing to me
He stole my soul and set it free
Sad my heart because of this
'Tis not my soul -
But the angel I miss . . .

Lisa Bristow

WHO!

Consider the rose, then tell me who conceived a flower
so fair to view?

Whose touch devised the satin-skin which guards the
fragrant heart within?

What Alchemist with her imbued the power sweet
perfume to exude?

Who makes the morning air transpose fresh dewdrops
on her to repose?

The elegance, the form devine,
That accolade dear Lord is thine!

Leonard Muscroft

SAD

Winter's Iron Maiden hold
Clamps darkness round my mind and soul

Spring's light heart hands back the key
To freedom and to sanity

Summer's warmth brings forth my pen
And inspiration flows again

Autumn glory tends to hide
The trepidation deep inside

Heralding the encroaching pain
Of incarceration again

Marion Evans

GIVE AND TAKE

The love of a man
Is to understand
And hold you
Near to his heart.
To care, and caress,
Nearly always say 'Yes'
Pay you lots of attention
From the start.

The love of a woman
Is to need her man,
Try to please him
All she can.
Love him, spoil him,
Come what may.
Nearly always agree
With what he has to say.

The conclusion is
To give and take.
It's surprising what
A difference it makes.

Sheila Hardwick

AN OLDER GENERATION

Old ladies with twinkling eyes,
Stiff of joint, but quick of mind.
Old men recalling memories of days long past,
When wars were won and battles lost.

Grandmas who have time to listen,
And perhaps sweets hidden in her bag.
Grandads who remember childhood games
And long forgotten nursery rhymes.

Crotchety old dears with sharp tongues
Condemning as thoughtless, the youth of today
Wistful old men wishing
They were young with all today's advantages.

These are the old people of today
Of yesterday and years gone by,
Will we - the youth of now
Be the same when we are old.

J M Tyler

EARTHBOUND

High, tethered, painted face in flight
Free with high wind above hot sands,
But only as free as my hands
That control it with will and might.

Thoughts flying free - not given birth -
Dreams fading in a darkened mind,
Ideas that will not unwind
Must, as the kite, return to Earth.

Our haltered spirits yearn to go
Where love and joy and peace abound.
But not till death can they be found;
Life pegs our tethers here below.

Tightfast hope is the only string
That keeps our aching souls alive,
While weary bodies can survive
Sure that winter brings new spring.

David Sewell Hawkins

THE PASSING OF THE NATION'S FAVOURITE GRANDMOTHER
(A remembrance of a fantastic life - 1900 -2002)

As a little child she was brought up in the North,
Little realising just how far she would go forth.
As a teenager she nursed casualties of the Great War,
Even then a sense of duty came to the fore.

Wooed and won by a Prince who was shy,
She vowed her Bertie was the man she'd stand by.
Married her Prince and bore two daughters,
Entered Royal life like a lamb to the slaughter.

Never really wanted to be the number one Royal,
But the Abdication threw her plans into turmoil.
Crowned in Westminster Abbey alongside the new King,
She accepted her destiny and grasped the ring.

Then war came again and the bombing began,
She became a great comfort in a war-ravaged land.
When the Palace was bombed she said with good grace,
'At least now I can look the East End in the face.'

Then the King died and she was so forlorn,
Didn't really want to carry on alone.
Churchill went to her and wove his magic,
Told her things weren't really that tragic.

She came out of mourning and began to be seen,
As a tower of strength to the nation and our Queen.
Everywhere she went she spread warmth and light,
People travelled for miles to see the sight.

Now that she's gone and can't be replaced,
Her lust for life and living we have to retrace.
The nation will mourn her for a long time to come,
Miss her sense of adventure, laughter and fun.

David Muncaster

Untitled

In my minds eye
    I can see
The kind of youth
    I used to be
Bit of a lad
    football mad
But educated - No!

Mathematics, science
    history
All a bit of
    a mystery
But playing football
    which I liked
And fifty thousand
    pounds a match
    Alright!

Can't spell or read
    but I can count
When I get my pay
    know the exact amount
For playing an hour
    and a half
Very trying on
    the calf.

So if my wage
    wasn't right
Like the others
    I could go on strike.

Cost ten million
    pounds to buy
Worth every penny
    you can bet
It's me, what puts
    the ball in the net.

Don't like getting
    on a plane
Me, I'd rather
    go by train.

But being a footballer
    first class
Take a pill
    shut my eyes
As we travel
    through the sky.

Maybe I should
    have studied more!

Frank Oldfield

MUD-PUDDLE CHILD

You were a mud-puddle child when I met you
messy child, dirty from head to toe
loved splashing in mud-puddles
hated splashing in mud-puddles
you had to get clean
you tried to get clean
you showered
you bathed
but wherever you went there was still a mud-puddle
you never saw the signs
never saw the mud-puddle
messy child, dirty from head to toe
tried to get clean
never got clean
you showered
you bathed
but fell in another mud-puddle
and were never again seen.

Trish Walton

NORTH YORKSHIRE

Silent and strange were the uplands
    Once all the sheep had gone
Not to the whistling shepherd but
    Gone to the man with the gun
Whilst down the dale a field of kale
    Stood rotting in the sun
And pastures where prize cattle grazed
    Were left unkempt - forlorn.

Farm gates chain-locked, red warnings set
    Fell walkers frowned upon
The dreaded foot and mouth had closed
    Near all the footpaths down
Sickly smells hung in cobbled streets
    From funeral pyres burning
And smoke discoloured forest firs
    Like the wilderness returning.

But nature can't be shackled
    New life has filled the void
Wild flowers some kinds forgotten
    Now here to be enjoyed
Forest deer drawn by sweet moor grass
    Have thrived and multiplied.
Walkers too fill village inns
    Where farmers sat and cried.

J Ellison

A Touch Of Dutch

A gentleman called into college one day to ask for some
                                       lessons in Dutch -
He said he was able and willing to pay (provided
                                       the fees were not much)
'I'll shortly be moving to Holland and so I'll need to be able to speak,
But only these phrases I've written, you know -
                         it shouldn't take more than a week!'
The lecturer summoned was Hans Van der Maal,
                         who looked at the gentleman's list:
The phrases he read weren't exactly banal, and so he began to insist:
'I don't understand how you plan to get by with phrases
                                 like these written down . . . '
'I'll pay you to *teach* me and not question why'
                 (the student was starting to frown).

The lecturer silently scanned through the page where
                           phrases were written in black:
The first one was: 'Don't get me into a rage - now, do
                           as I say and come back!'
The next: 'Let's go out' and 'It's time to come in,' then:
'Go on, your dinner is there'
'Oh, do stop your yapping, I can't stand the din!'
                     'You know you can't sit in that chair.'
'Do you want a biscuit? I've told you, don't snatch -
conduct yourself properly, please!'
'When you're in the house I don't want you to scratch -
come here, I believe you have fleas!'
'Now stay in the kitchen - leave Pussy alone:
I mean it, stop teasing the cat!'
'Be good and I'll give you a nice, juicy bone, *no*, sexy beast,
stop doing that!'
The ultimate phrase was: 'No - out you must go,
I've told you so often before,
The yard is the place for that, surely you know, not here
                           on the carpeted floor!'

The student, now mollified, gave him a smile and
                      started to try and explain:
'I'm going to Holland to work for a while -
I doubt if I'll come back again:
The house I have rented is one on its own and no other people live near,
But I don't intend to be really alone - I hope that I make myself clear?
As soon as I move a companion I'll bring . . .
                      (the lecturer now was agog!)
I'm planning to buy, when I go in the spring, a very
                      young Netherlands dog'
The student continued: I'll train him, you see, and
                      make him obey and be good.
So I must learn all of these phrases to be quite certain
                      I'll be understood -
That puppy of course, will be Dutch, born and bred,
so Dutch is the language he'll know,
And *those* are the phrases, I've already said, I hope
                      I'll have learned when I go!'

Rosemary Yvonne Vandeldt

OUR PAT

My sister means the world to me,
My everything, my all,
She makes me laugh, she makes me cry,
She is my heart and soul.

Her name it is Patricia,
Everyone calls her Pat,
She has another middle name,
But I won't mention that.

She is a special person,
With a special quality,
You only have to meet her
And it is plain to see.

She's loving and she's caring,
Kind and honest too,
Giving so much to others,
Selfless through and through.

Many times we act like twins,
Though she is a bit older than me,
We have a special closeness,
Just like telepathy.

We often wear the same clothes,
Our thoughts are much the same,
I ring her up, she's phoning me,
It happens again and again.

There is no better sister,
You can search far and wide,
I love our Pat with all my heart,
Where she is locked inside.

Kathleen Hackleton

SEA GRAVES

Within the ocean buried deep,
Lie souls of sailors fast asleep,
Above their grave the waves may roar,
But peace pervades the ocean floor.
Their coffins lie in silver sand
Untouched by time or human hand.
Long ships, galleons, ships of the line,
Who sank in sea fights at a time
When battles raged across the foam,
Defending those they loved at home.
Liners, yachts and submarines
Once sailed out with hopeful dreams.
The sea laid wreaths of waving fronds,
Briny jewels deck the mounds
Of broken hulls, crustaceans cling to sunken decks,
The sea builds shrines from hollow wrecks,
Do not disturb these Cathedrals deep,
The hallowed halls where sailors sleep.

Pauline M Parlour

WHO WOULD LIKE A TOY BOY

Alas, I'm not so young
Except within my heart
Would like to have a toy boy
But don't know where to start.

I'd like him strong and healthy:
Fastidious he must be,
Treat me kind and gentle,
Sometimes flatter me.

We'd visit places of interest,
Dine out once or twice
Have a picnic in the park
Would be oh so nice.

Time is running out I fear.
Will anyone hear my plea?
There must be a toy boy out there
Who'll take a chance with me.

Kathleen Wheeler

THE GARDEN OF LOVE

The fortune of Kings couldn't alter the way that the winds blow,
A will made of steel couldn't alter the flow of the brine,
The wonders of earth couldn't give back new life to the roses,
Or bring back the ripples now passed 'neath the bridges of time.
The strength of a Regiment can't hold back the march of the seasons,
Or coax back the sap that's deserted the leaf and the bud,
But the heart recalls echoes of joy, like a voice from the mountain,
And returns every rose in full bloom to the garden of love.

Gillian Walsh

LIFE'S VALUE?

So, wherein lies the value of our life?
To this a *two-fold* answer we must give.

That vital, free and immaterial force,
That animating thrust which is the source,
The fountain-head of *being* for us all,
We pass from living cell to living cell.
Its origin unknown, we but transmit
The 'principle' we cannot yet create:
Whereon, the use to which it can be put
Defines its worth, (a worth like that
Of currency, utility the key!)

But life has value over this, for we
Do more than just exist on earth, we dwell.
We make 'the moral choice,' (for good or ill.)
Though 'what' and 'who' we are is vague at first,
While changes in our human form are vast,
Mysteriously, our 'Self' remains the same!

The paradox is clear. Our *changing* frame
Continuing identity upholds
Throughout our years, as youth to age unfolds.
Yet humankind inevitably fades,
Then falls to sweeps of Nature's scything blade.
Autonomy no longer in our grasp,
Our 'Self' escapes, at last, the body's clasp.

Our *'brain'* and *'mind'* express profound belief
In *'vital'* and *'experiential'* life.
And maybe we do wrong to separate
These two, as moral challenges dictate.
But *needs,* from embryo to personhood,
Require we value 'life' in dual mode!

John M Beazley

TIME

Be still my restless soul
The time will surely come
When you will be forever free
Free to reach your goal.

You watch the seasons
Of time, and remember!
How your heart raced
Forward into spring.

Now as autumn approaches
Thoughts come of the dreams
That were never realised,
And you fold them away.

Your heart still knows
The feeling of love
And the surge in the mind
To fulfil it!

But the body has slowed
To a gentle pace
And now can only
Watch the race.

Things that were static
Now hit the floor
And you don't see the wall
When you walk through the door.

The laces in shoes
Get further away
And you have to get close
To hear what folk say.

But you are my soul, forever young!
And ready to face the brand new day.

Joan May Wills

THE TRUTH

And as we use our wit and guile,
To carry us through the many miles.
We enter, and look upon your face,
Loving and kind, full of grace.
How do you know our deepest minds?
For answers we are here to find.
'Look not at yourself look at the youth,
For there you will find honesty and truth.'
But truth, is never easy on the mind,
And love sometimes makes us blind.
Take a step back and grab a rest,
For he is not here to judge or test.
Just a gateway for you and me,
So all is clear in what we see.
Refreshed we carry on, and look no more,
Enlightened, we turn and close the door.

Dawn Graham

A LITTLE BIRD

On Tuesday a little bird we found;
It could not fly, just hop around,
So seeing she could hardly stand
We took this little bird in hand.

Seeing this lovely bird in pain
We thought we'd get her well again.
On Wednesday she appeared alright;
We kept her always in our sight.

Thursday around the yard she was seen,
Looking better and starting to preen.
She had water to drink and crumbs to eat,
Then she'd sit down beside us at our feet.

Friday she was becoming tame,
Yet this little beauty was still lame.
We saw the heaving of her breast;
To try to save her we did our best.

On Friday sitting here in our flat,
To our back door came neighbour, Pat,
The little bird nestling in her hand;
Pat had found her lying, unable to stand.

In my hand she gasped for breath;
As I laid her down, came her death,
Wide open beak, stretched out legs
Our beautiful blackbird now lay dead.

Oh, little bird, you had to die;
You would never have learned to fly.
So little time you had here on earth,
But we thank the Lord for your birth.

Francis Allen

STARLIGHT WONDER

I stood in darkness 'neath the silent boughs
of shadowy trees and whispering leaves,
surrounded by blackness,
listening, in a dream, to the rippling, unseen stream.
The velvet darkness of the heavenly arch
caressed me, as I stood, waiting, in that wood.

And as I watched, a silver prick of light
the darkness broke. I laughed with great delight.
This cosmic gift my hands stretched out to touch,
to hold it in my hands - I wanted to so much!

The starlight then began to grow.
Myriad star pricks in space where fixed.
My star glowed.
A shine of stars adorned the arch with sparks
from the glittering mass of living and dead orbs.
With transfixed eyes I wondered at the skies.

Then from the silence came the breath of peace.
I knew, for all time, love would never cease.
That moment all my dreams and hopes took wing -
a moment held forever on a silver string.

Sheila E Harvey

THE AIR HELD CHANGE!

A young September sunny day
When brightness glowing was so clear,
The air held change that found its way
While souls looked up and cried in fear.

Then waves of shock and disbelief
Disaster struck from dark reveal,
Without concern for distant grief
Or time of pain and pain that's real.

So flames of death and clouds of smoke
Engulfing life reached to the sky,
More evil than the evil yoke
That falls on love to make love cry.

True breath of help it breathed with care
And so the brave they did not creep,
But daylight heard their final prayer
And sleep now holds them while we weep!

Unfriendliness had been unfurled
And tallness fell so painfully,
Then stirring sounds throughout the world,
What kind of heart wills this to be?

Dust covered forms moved to the light
While many thought it was the end,
Then when some clearness came to sight
Sweet love was offered as a friend.

Emotion flowed, all mourning cried,
Seek out the roots where rests the blame!
For nations' hearts are side by side
With love to light the Freedom Flame!

Peter James O'Rourke

A World Around Us

Winter just a brief pause
Negative to sudden change
From the overcast shadows
That makes its own photograph of enlightenment
That comes into being
Of white enrichment

Down to its muted sounds
To our mind's own motivations
Rich to that gilded rose
Of nature which becomes
Ours of seasonal offering
From a mirrored landscape

To a world around us.

Roger Thornton

CAUSE OF DEATH

The cat sits on the mat and purrs,
Contented, happy, fat cat,
Sleek fur shining in the sunlight,
Pleased with life, she falls asleep to dream.

The cat sits on the floor
Outside the bathroom door.
Doesn't like being shut out
She believes in her furry right to roam.

The cat lies on the mat and shrieks,
No midwife to ease her pain,
She does it alone,
Surveying the new lives with pride,
No one there to share the joy.

The cat prowls hungrily outside the door
Her kittens now number four,
Two are no more,
The matted fur doesn't gleam any more.

The cat lies on the bloodied mat
And yowls desperately.
One little scrap of fur remains,
To seek the warmth and nourishment
She can no longer provide.

Tattered, threadbare, skeletal cat
Can't hang on, now the water's gone
From the kitchen sink
And so she prepares to die.

The cat sits docile in the refuge's cage,
As freedom bearing humans hover outside,
Her babies and hopes died because of a human,
She will not be owned again.

Clare Anne Lewis

BLUE GLASS ON A GREY DAY

Sitting alone
In this Gallery cafe
On this grey
Manchester morning
It caught my eye
On the waitress's tray
Without any warning
Just a small blue bottle
But to me a bit of magic
It caught the light
And I knew I had to have it
She looked at me in surprise
When I pointed out its beauty
Offered it to me
With such a smile
Before she went off duty
So here I sit at my table
Still life with blue bottle.

Elizabeth Thorpe

MY SON, MY LOVE, WHERE ARE YOU?

At seventeen
I married your father
an arranged marriage.
What could I expect?

As a wife
and then a mother
one by one
and then four altogether.

You are the eldest
you are my flesh
you are my first friend
you were cultivated within my womb.

My parents divorced.
Your father divorced me.
He kept you away from me.
How much I miss you.

I want you to stay with me
Instead,
you asked me to take your younger brother and sisters to run away.

I really want to set you free from your father's captivity
but where are you?
My dear son,
my soul.

Mei Yuk Wong

A Day In The Sun

This July day was destined to be hot
A cloud in the sky there was not.

The sun became hotter and hotter
No hat upon my head, but I did not bother.

Walking over hills the trees were few
There was no shade while admiring the view.

Plenty of drinks and food so well watered and fed
The bald patch on my head now very warm and red.

When the sun began to set in the west
I started to shiver, still only in my vest.

Feeling really ill now for no apparent reason
The sun is leaving me and it feels like winter's season.

Extra clothes could not stop the shivering
It became obvious it was sunstroke I was suffering.

A day walking in the hot sun
A white hat helps to enjoy the summer's fun.

Brian Bates

NOW IT'S FOR REAL

It has always been you, right from the start
You came into my life, and stole my heart
When I looked into your deep blue eyes
The love that I felt could not be disguised.

Take me to heaven with your magical touch
This time it's for real, I love you so much.

You held me close, it felt so good
You made me feel like a woman should
Protected, desired, alive and new
My Darling, my heart I give to you.

Take me to heaven with your magical touch
This time it's for real, I love you so much.

Forever, together, just you and me,
We'll show the whole world that we're meant to be
I thought that I had been in love before
But now I know I really am, now I am sure.

Take me to heaven with your magical touch,
This time it's for real, I love you so much.

Maggy Copeland

DEMOLITION
(The Mayfield High Rise Flats 2001)

The yellow crane with its awesome claw,
Dislodges, vibrates,
Penetrates, violates,
Bricks crash as they plummet to the ground,
Spiralling out of control to terra-firma,
Whilst plunging and tumbling blocks of concrete split apart,
Lying fragmented, strewn upon the ground,
Cast aside like an out-dated garment,
Midst mangled window frames,
And jagged glass splinters and shards.

The ousted inhabitants memories are buried,
Homes are torn apart,
In the remnants of partial living spaces,
Are revealed assorted floral wallpapers,
Debris segments cling precariously to intact floor sections,
Whilst furniture that once gave comfort to a weary body,
Lies upside down and left behind,
Along with old boilers, cookers and heaters,
All are strewn across the site,
Amidst trees uprooted and lying horizontal.

Paving slabs on which many families trod,
And reclaimed wood from the premises,
Are sold to those seeking home and garden improvements,
Who wheel their assorted 'goodies' eagerly to their homes,
Excavations provide man-made mountains of soil,
Lorries full to the brim of earth and rubble,
Make constant journeys to empty their load in some unknown habitat,

The name of the game is demolition,
The future reclaims the recent past,
Erasing it completely from view.

The landmark will soon be barren as modernisation makes its mark,
The once sturdy high-rise flats disintegrate and the area
                                          is left desecrated.

Ann G Wallace

WE ARE WHAT WE ARE

We are what we are and that's it
We are the genes we inherit
We are just what the sower sow
We have no choice where we will grow
To be successful or misfit.

We blossom where chance will permit
To live in shade or land sunlit
In stature tall or stature low
We are what we are.

But when in company we drift
The choice is ours to stay or quit
The wise will know the time to go
The fool stays on to his sorrow
We become what we must admit
We are what we are.

K W Benoy

THE GIFT

What gift can I give you this Christmas
A gift - what should it be?
Once the gift of a new-born child
That all the world could see
But like all things that grow - you've grown
In a world that's different from then
A world of I need, of I want and greed
All things sought after by men
So whatever you're after this Christmas
I wonder
Will that brightly coloured tinsel wrapped package
Truly satisfy your need.

So I've thought and my gift
So perfectly simple in every way
Is what I'm now offering you
It is today
I see you smile
Yes, strange as it may seem
The past now known, a future yet to come
But the gift of today
Yes, that will be the present
It's the real gift
A truly special one.

Katherine Parker

WORDS OF LOVE

Poignant memories of St Valentine
Cards of mystery arousing hearts that pine
Lifting emotions like bubbling champagne
Romance fills the air, love is found again
Yes, 14th February hearts throb and passions flow,
Did you receive one, I do hope so!

Stella Bush-Payne

Uninvited Guest

Sparkling glasses, gleaming silver
Tall red candles softly shimmer
On fine cream linen small brown prints
Meander
At ground level Stella purrs
Innocently.

Brenda Dove

SWEET MEADOWS

One morn, I stepped out of my cottage,
looking at the freshly fallen raindrops,
glistening in the morning sunshine, like
thousands of jewels sent down from heaven,
on this sweet meadow.
Listen! I hear the song of a skylark
across the coppice. Wait, what stirred
inside it? Mother rabbit pops out with
her off-springs, behind her a fox,
looking for a quick meal.
In the trees a song thrush sends forth
its beautiful melody. All this is laid
out before you, if only you will be quiet
and wait for God's creatures to appear
On returning from the meadow,
I spy cheeky Charly, my blackbird,
sparrows and later, from my cottage window,
partaking of a drink from the bird bath,
a squirrel,
what joy this brings me.
These are all God's creatures and
I thank Him for creating them.

Maureen Margaret Huber

DELUGE OF DEATH

Noah saved his people from the Flood,
Took warning from Jaweh, his God, his creator.
Obediently he built his ark of gopher wood,
Kept every pair of beasts from ape to alligator.
In the year 2002 prophecy does not unnerve.
Natural disasters bring mammoth tides.
We plunder the Earth as an infinite reserve,
Ignore tornadoes, arid deserts, mud-slides,
Melting of ice caps as water overflows.
Money is God. Omniscience makes no plan.
We pollute the Earth, global warming grows.
Species die out. What is the span of man?
When London lies beneath the sea
Who will then our Noah be?

Jane England

WAIT AWHILE

Wait awhile and listen
A solitary scream unleashed
Silent in the cruel sun.
That faith,
Enraged by hopeless loss made
Death and martyrs of children.

Wait awhile and see
A single tear fall
Soft upon the dusty ground.
That love,
Engulfed by jealous hate made
Dying seem worthwhile.

Wait awhile and hear
A solemn voice sing out
Sweet among the guns.
That hope,
Ember-like within a burning grief banished
Dialogue and reason.

Wait awhile should tireless enemies demur

Love from out the swelling rage might
Innocents from pain set free and
Voiceless choirs with golden notes
Embroider then pure harmony from
Shame.

Ruth Kavanagh

DREAM OF INDIA

Come with me to the land of dreams
Where waterfalls and mountain streams
Where roams the tiger of great delight
Men even fear him of his great might.

The tiger walks with stilth and grace
His eyes burn like gold in his face
He hides up in the grass so tall his stripes
Are black no one knows he's there at all.

Elephants roam this land when they call it's like a band
The Rajah rides on elephants back across the forest floor they track
The tiger walks with stilth and grace.

Hoping to catch a glimpse of him once more
He hides once more across the land
Silent and quick he makes his way
Up in the mountain back to his cave.

The tiger is a graceful beast but hunted
Now and ever more
So men can have his skin to lay
Upon on their floor.

Elizabeth A Wilkinson

JESSIE HAM

Today we lost Jessie Ham,
Such a modest man,
He's found a union in the sky,
Which miners join when they die.

The years that numbered his life,
Were of trouble and strife,
He was known as Jess the brave,
For inspiration he gave.

His blue scarred body told the tale,
Of sweat and toil under dale,
With mates of blackened faces,
He worked in confined spaces.

A Davey lamp hung on a prop,
A pony named Pop
And a canary in a cage,
Helped to earn a living wage.

Friends rallied round
When he was hurt underground,
A sum was raised,
Which left him dazed!

For this gift of love,
He thanked the Lord above,
For a God fearing man,
Was Jessie Ham.

Passing events, long since gone,
Were times he called upon,
To help in later age,
To read life's last sober page.

His epitaph should read,
'This man was born to lead.'
So please God, bless,
Dear old Jess.

Alan Dawes

THE LAST RESTING PLACE

Everything was ready. Everyone had taken their place.
There were those who had arrived the night before.
Making sure to be near to you as possible,
When you passed by on your last journey for the state.

Standard lowered, coffin in place. Places . . . place . . .
A word to be heard many times repeated, in the hours to come.
As you moved away, it came to me, with some emotion,
Though I am no great follower of the Royalist cause.
You were going away and never would return.

The members of your household staff, sharing a dual burden.
Goodbye to you Mam. Sorry to see you go.
Now the Job Centre beckons.
Fifty years of faithful service must count for something.
Last employer? HRH, sorry, I will be unable to provide
                                        a reference from her.

The Catafalque . . . Now that's a word to get to grips with.
Though I doubt that bench or plinth would do.
You can just hear it now in the local,
Didn't she look upon . . . my round.

The boys looked the part as they took their turn . . . their place.
One for each corner. A very deep loss for the one who would be King.
Why did you have to die Grandma? Who do I turn to now?

Had it been up to me, your service would have been held in
The Great Hall. Simple and to the point.
The Abbey . . . gilt and ornate. The crowned heads,
The Managers of the State . . . throw in a bard or two.

Outside the car is waiting. Take your time. Last words have been said.
Time for bed. Your beloved guards hand you over to the men in black.
Next stop Windsor. The family will gather round . . .
Tell you how much you will be missed.
What else is there to say? Goodbye, the end . . .
However one tries, embellishments galore can never change what is . . .

And that is . . . the End really is the End.

G J Cayzer

SLOW DOWN

Hustle and bustle of every day life,
Tourists adding to the struggle.
There's every kind of fashion statement here.
Purposefully striding along,
Reaching for ultimate destinations.
No time to sit and savour lunch,
Every step means a mouthful of pleasure,
Eating as you walk a habit.
Slow down, you are rushing your life away,
Take time to stand back and question.

Angela Pritchard

YOU WERE . . .

You were the ocean,
I was the wave,
You were the laughter,
I thought never would fade.
You were the bridge,
So sturdy and firm,
And you were the teacher,
From whom I would learn.
You were the friend,
Through the good and the bad,
The one to remember,
All the fun times we'd had.
And now as it comes,
When we must forever part,
You know you will always,
Remain in my heart.

Laura Nixon (15)

SOLITUDE AND TEARS

O' solitude, if I must with thee dwell,
    Now alone, I walk with soul apprest,
I will, I must these weary fetters break -
    If only for her sake,
To what may lie beyond sets my star,
    My tender heart could to itself confess,
    Saddened with endless disquiet in my breast,
With yearning desire, and lips apart -
    I turned and saw that answering look again,
    And stayed my hurried footsteps, till the parting came.

Her parting gesture, her subdued farewell,
    When day and night I have cried all in vain,
    And both have punished ourselves, with the pain,
We broke our faith, and strangely slipped apart,
    I had a dim belief that it would be,
    A better thing for her, a blessed thing for me,
My thoughts and absence may return to nought,
    Unfriended, unkissed, comfort shut me out,
    And there was nothing left to talk about.

Nothing lies beyond but memories and tears
    I looked at the picture of her in my mind
    Still followed in her wake, though far behind,
Will absence heal me, when its shade doth end,
    No laughter, no music, no voice to say goodbye,
    Thus we parted, she and I,
If I could comfort me, I know not how,
    For I have nothing left to long for now,
O' how much more could costly parting buy,
    If not a pledge, if not a kiss, or failing that, a sigh.

John Leighton

STILL HIBERNATING?

I waken from my winter doze
In the rocking chair before the fire.
And through the window I espy
Brave snowdrops peeping through the snow
And if I plan a summer show
Of colour, then I know
That seedlings, compost-cushioned,
Coaxed with warmth must soon be sown,
But this gardener will await
Until the cold north winds abate.

Muriel Berry

My Valentine

My eyes have seen some amazing sights,
Like the days changing into nights,
The tide coming in and going out,
The children laughing and running about,
But they haven't seen anything more beautiful than you.

My lips have touched milk and honey,
Sweet and sour chips curry and rice,
They have kissed loads of money,
Which was quite nice,
But they haven't touched anything sweeter than you.

My hands have had lots of jewels to hold,
Rubies, diamonds, sapphires, silver and gold,
Medallions, chains, bracelets, lockets and rings,
They have held lots of beautiful things,
But they haven't held anything more precious
Or valuable than you.

Michael McNulty

HAPPY AND WARM

This is about writing a poem
the way that I do.
Line composition flows repetitive
one-two, one-two.
Running one-two-three-four
the poem grows a little more.
If stuck at five and six
skip to seven and eight.
The thing is looking good
it is going great.
Go back later to five and six
inspiration will get you out of a fix.
Now you are doing well
as the words on the page start to swell.
This is how it can be done
put pen to paper, have some fun.
Poetry in its best form
will keep you happy and warm.

S Glover

MUM

If I could hope for anything,
This is what my wish would be,
To be as good and kind a Mum,
As Mum is now to me.
She's always there if I need her,
And in times past, so true,
To give advice, a comforting word,
And problems then, seem few.
The years are passing by now,
And still we're best of friends,
A telephone chat, a joke, a laugh
And sometimes, to make amends.
If I can be a mum like that,
And at times it's quite a task,
Mum, all that you have taught me -
Keep showing me, that's all I ask!
The children think she's wonderful,
'Dear Nana, come and play,
Today, we'll all be cowboys.'
They cheerfully 'whoop' and say
Poor Mum, stands quite bewildered,
As they dress her up with glee,
Oh help, just think in times to come,
That person could be me!

Sheryll Janet Hubbard

MY PERFECT HEAVEN

It's a coming of a new age they say,
New world with different people in it.
A start for mankind and alike, my perfect heaven.

I turn on the axis of the earth with my head held high.
I look for answers in the eyes of others that stand before me,
My perfect heaven.

Beautiful noises ring out with a deafening sense of liberation,
Across the land down through drenched forests and valleys,
Those noises are sounds of pleasure, sounds of my perfect heaven.

So come and join others and me,
Step into the light, make yourself known and be counted,
For now is the time to let go, and join me in my perfect heaven.

Jonty Holt

STUNNED BY IT ALL
(Bitter disappointment)

I went to a meeting the other day,
Expectant and hopeful of what they would say
About houses in Rainford they wrongly condemned.
Thinking this error they would surely amend.

At last! Thought I a definite conclusion,
But who's kidding who?
'Twas just another delusion. Two minutes I think was
All that it took to bring up this issue and dismiss from the book,
Deferred until August . . .
Or was it September?
I was so stunned I can hardly remember.

Two long years we've suffered and fretted,
Waiting and wondering how our homes will be vetted.
One voice and one only was raised in concern for people
Who sadly will swiftly learn that their housing committee
Just couldn't care less and are in little hurry to clear up the mess.
I longed to tell them, 'This issue's *a must!*'
But . . . all I could do was leave in *disgust*.

Florence Taylor

ANONYMOUS II

The puppy ran from man.
Amber eyes agonised
Body beaten through hate.
Was this the puppy's fate?
No one saw it cry,
No one heard it die,
Help came too late.

Pauline Scragg

JUST A GAME

The bitter-sweet of win defeat,
When luck can take a hand,
When expectations can't be met,
The fans won't understand,
On the day, the heroes made,
But next week out of favour,
The conflicts and the skirmishes,
An atmosphere to savour,
Just a game is often heard,
From those who fail to see,
The power of support for club,
Can split a family,
A sport that breaches barriers,
Of class and generation,
That lifts the players of the sport,
To heights of veneration,
Should we say, 'It's just a game,'
Or show consideration,
To sport that wields such power in life,
And earns such dedication.

Martin Jordan

WHERE LIVES A PRAYER FOR YOU

So now you wake in paradise
'Neath skies of eternal love
A realm of spiritual freedom
Where every soul has stood

Its light is your deliverance
Its faith is now your throne
Although you live in its belief
Our hearts shall be your home

Thus our hearts are always open
Where once your presence grew
Your memories grace this humble world
Where lives a prayer for you

David Bridgewater

LONG DISTANCE

Emotion builds inside as I wait for the instrument of torture to ring,
When at last it does, I pounce, almost dropping the receiver.
All day I've been anxious to hear the sexy voice I know so well.
Your deep, rich sonorous tones just make my heart sing.

Being apart from you is sheer hell,
Your voice, warm and loving is a thread I cling to.
A link to the one person who marks my whole world,
Who reads me, who knows me so damn well.

You ask how I feel? Can't you tell?
I'm sure you hear the pain, the loneliness in my voice,
Just as I catch the longing in yours,
The knowledge that without me, you're just an empty shell.

Right now, what you're saying is immaterial,
Your voice is all I want to hear, it's home.
How can a mixture of resonance, pitch and tone,
Conjure up a hearth, bricks and mortar so real?

As I curl up on the sofa, phone cradled to my ear,
Melting into the warmth you transmit,
The dread of the call ending looms larger,
The words 'goodbye' not those I want to hear.

I dredge up inane topics, useless chatter,
I can tell by your volume you're aware of my tricks,
But the strength, the love in your voice,
Lets me know that it doesn't matter.

Tells me, you feel the same, don't want the contact to end,
That certainty makes me feel so secure,
Our feelings marry, reflecting the other,
There's no ambiguities, no mistakes we can send.

A glance at the clock tells me we've been on far too long,
A cloaking sadness descends - you feel it too,
We hedge, we avoid, till you prove what I know,
You'll be first to break our intimacy, I'm not that strong.

An hour later , I'm still staring at the object so silent,
Wishing with all my heart you were here in the room,
Picturing you all those miles away, all alone,
Heart breaking, emotions so vulnerable, so spent.

Patricia Cunningham

DYN HYBYS

At first, the bearers staggered under his weight
but then, the coffin got lighter and lighter
so they said
and a herd of cows stampeded in a field
near the graveyard
terrified

what remains for us
is a brown and white photograph
of a dark, heavy-lidded man
a book in his right hand
sealed with seven seals

> *I conjure thee, thou great and potent Prince . . .*

once a year
when he carried the book to the mountain
to 'his' stone
the skies darkened
over the Vale of Caio
thunder rolled, as he opened it
and an angel proclaimed in a loud voice

> *Who is worthy to open the book*
> *and loose the seals thereof?*

now 'his' stone
a dark and smooth boulder
lies wounded, cut into
by local people
in search for its powers

so

should you enter the Vale of Caio
remember to look for the grave of
Dr John Harries of Pantcoy
medicine man, astrologer and conjuror
but beware!

do not cut down an elder tree
because
a death in your house will be

Alfa

STREET NAMES IN FORMBY VILLAGE

Surrounded by farmland, pine forest
And a stretch of treacherous coast,
Host to an early Viking settlement.
Can boast of the first lifeboat station
A gun fired from the old lighthouse
Ship in distress.
Men clinging to the rigging of a wreck
Half-frozen and falling from the mast
Helped by villagers, to safety at last.
Boat rowed ashore in days that are past
Lifeboat Road.

Priest House built in the reign of William and Mary
Had an underground tunnel to a look-out point
Worshippers warned to escape from harm
The alarm raised in nick of time, again and again
From the street whose present day name
Is Watchyard Lane.

Death of a priest hiding in a Priest Hole
To escape from Cromwell and his men
A haunting ghost story is told
Of the road,
Priesthouse Lane.

Some strange sounding names
Recalling the past.

Freda Grieve

FAITH

I walked along a country lane
in a place where I had never been.
Towards a lonely sea-washed shore
(And few had come that way before).
There stood a chapel old and small,
it's spare-framed Minister leaned on the wall.
A well used prayer book in his hand,
he stood near the graves by the rocky strand.
From the threadbare cassock, old as he,
his hoary head looked out to sea
for a fishing boat set out to roam,
which never more would come home.

He turned and slowly walked away
as he had done near every day
for twenty years, since she sailed away
taking his three sons out of the bay.
Out into the gathering storm,
their father in the chapel at home.
Through the familiar door he went,
to kneel and pray till strength was spent.

D H Taylor

How Lovely

Sitting in the garden, dreaming.
    The hot sun touching my face.
Listening to the sounds all around me,
    Thinking how lovely, is this place.

Birds are singing in the branches,
    Bees buzzing in the lavender bush.
Butterflies flitting from flower to flower
    Always in a rush.

Scents of different flowers,
    Roses, carnations and sweet peas.
Tomatoes ripening in the greenhouse,
    How lovely, to see all these.

In the distance, church bells are ringing
    Calling us all to prayer.
Or maybe, it could be a wedding,
    A bride, with flowers in her hair.

We didn't have a good winter,
    It was cold, windy and wet.
How we looked forward to this lovely summer
    The sunshine, we hoped we would get.

As I sit here, still dreaming.
    I think of the days long gone by
When we both sat here together,
    How lovely, just you and I.

The moonlight will soon be upon us,
    The sky full of twinkling stars.
A sunset to light up the heavens,
    How lovely, all these things are.

The summer will soon turn again to winter,
    We must make the most of these days,
And pray to our Father who gave us
    These blessings, in so many ways.

Joan Smith

CUERDEN PARK

Tall trees of larch and pine
clothe the hills of Cuerden Park.
Grassy swards of bluebells and buttercups,
where one hears no dog's angry bark.

A dog's delight and earthly paradise.
The ripple in the stream,
a soft sigh and rustle in the grass,
where no wind has been.

The river Lostock caressing the stepping stones
or rushing, bubbling and prancing,
with excited dogs as partners
to their spirited form of dancing.

Canada geese and goslings glide upon the lake.
The adult birds form a protective screen,
reminding us of convoy escorts
guarding their charges from submarines.

With bright eyes and head held high
a contented dog trots at my knee.
The ghosts of dogs long dead
follow as we tread homeward on the lea.

Robert Allen

THE MAD HATTER

I once was a hatter, most prosperous and sane,
I made hats all exquisite - some fancy, some plain.
There were hats for a wedding, with trimmings so fine
And hats for a funeral - that were almost divine.
A Fedora, a Beaver I made for a Diva,
A straw-boater - worn by a big city broker.
My straw, lace or gauze were met with applause,
When worn at Ascot or Henley or even indoors.
Yes! I once was a hatter, prosperous and sane,
But disaster has struck again and again.
No more 'tis the fashion to wear a chapeau
Or even buy one for a bride's trousseau.
And the guys no longer raise a hat to the gals,
Preferring to treat them like one of their pals.
If they cover their head, they choose a baseball cap
Wearing the peak at the front or side, or back.
Now I'm as mad as a March hare as you all can see
Driven to this by fashion's changing decree.
As I walk down the street no more prosperous or sane
I can hear people whisper again and again
'There goes the mad hatter who just wouldn't change.'
Yes! I'm mad and I fear there's no cure for my ills,
Except an overdose of some very strong pills.
Or unless fickle fashion brings back the bowler
Maybe I'll stay mad - and go live in Angola.

Margaret Hughes

MY MOTHER

You are dear and thoughtful in so many ways,
Mainly in what you say and do for me.
Every day that comes by will be adding
More love for you in my heart.
Mother, you are the perfect picture of love.

Caroline Ashton

NEW BABY

Wow, I can't wait,
I can't concentrate,
I can't sleep, can't eat
Not even my favourite treat.

I can't do my work at school
I'm just acting like a fool,
I can't write, I can't think
It's just that I can't do these things.

Wow, this is the day
I've been waiting since May,
Can't wait till mum gets here,
The hospital is quite near.

Yesterday was the day
It came in a glorious way,
With happiness and tears
For many, many years.

Matthew Ferguson (12)

The Woman In The Photograph

You may be an old flame
with a casket of dubious fame
so is your reappearance a ploy
or a natural joy.
Once the pain in my heart
made me think you were a tart
Luckily I was in my prime
but now due to the passage of time
Why should I have any shame
so again here you came
Asking me to pick up your glove
but is this really love?
For you may still be a little zany
but in terms of friends, do you really have any?
So ask yourself who is to blame
yet all the same
We could still be bliss
but now I will give it a miss.

James Ashworth

WITHIN THE FOREST OF PENDLE

I grew on Pendle's ancient hill
Roots planted firm and strong
A mighty oak tree standing there
Till one day came along
A strong north wind began to blow
To shake my leafy bough
An acorn falling to the ground
Produced a seed somehow
Its cup discarded slightly bruised
And yet it felt no pain
Silent in the dark it lay

Just waiting for the rain
When Mother Nature lent a hand
The shoot began to grow
With care and toil she lingered
In a fertile spot I know
Throughout the year it grew so strong
Producing sap and bark
That flourished in the summer sun
And slept when it went dark
Until at last a young tree stood
Nestling deep within the wood
Where root and branch and bough combine
To grow a tree so tall and fine
Within the Forest of Pendle.

David A Carter

Hope For The World

As we depart from winter to the life of spring
We mark the march of time
Welcoming another clime

Thankful in our hearts that for a short span
We are privileged as on this Earth we run
Time can be sold, but cannot be bought
Question? What have we wrought?
Is this happiness and peace?
That we have passed to our brother
Or disharmony passing just another grace

To another Millennium must be
Peace, harmony and love
Before we are returned to the source
To our creator and found wanting
Time ticks with the beat of our heart
Letting it fan the flames of our love

Give the Earth's children hope
Let our dreams be reality
Give them the peace and harmony
For what is sustenance to the body
If we do not feed the spirit of man also
For the uplifting of the spirit is its own healer

Anne E Marshall

OVER THE MOOR

Over the moor, not all that far
There is a place that I know,
With rolling hills, gentle and green.
The road twists and turns, this way and that,
As it takes me there, just down the road,
Not all that far, just *over the moor.*

With rivers flowing on their way,
My road twists and turns, this way and that.
As it takes me there, to this place, not far away,
Just down the road, and *over the moor.*

With fields so green, and woods so tall,
There is so much to see and do.
In this place, not far away,
Just down the road, and *over the moor.*

Trevor Howarth

GOING HOME

Turn right at the oak tree, then left at the stone
Carry on straight and hurry on home
Duck under the bridge and splash through the brook
Hang on to your hat, your bag and your book
Don't stay in the meadow, amongst the wild flowers
Five minutes will take quite a few of your hours
Look for your footprints, there since morn
Tread quickly the path by fields of corn
Skip, hop and then run down the grass covered track
Then burst through the door with . . .
'Hello Mum, I'm back!'

Olwyn Kershaw

SHE OF HEAVENS
(Dedicated to Anna)

The sun deprived of ardour
Sends still a clear beam through thinning cloud
Exchanges brightness with the air's lulling gust
The rose bush bending, melodiously
The atmosphere hails
A sisterly embrace.

Now it is that Creation's Princess
Leaves her slender chair
Abandoning splendour, ironies or levity
Like one clement, she comes down
To speak to man, her subject
Countering perversity.

With the border of her gown
Glowing starrily across the void
She soothes the suffering brow
Hers is an infinite spirit
The force ever peerless
Still granting calm and renewal
To our hearts, full as fools are.

Jason Redvers Latham

INCY TIPSY SPIDER

Incy tipsy spider lives in a dark cool cellar,
He really is the happiest, inebriated fellar.
As the brandy ages quietly, pungent fumes fill the air,
But this causes a great problem with Incy's little lair.
Instead of spinning his web in the customary manner
Incy cannot see that straight, so it looks just like a banner.
He gazes in admiration at his handiwork so fine,
Smacks his lips in anticipation of a meal of grubs divine.
All he needs to do now, is hang on good and tight
Happy in the knowledge that soon he'll get a bite.
He snoozes whilst he waits, until he feels a little movement
Then opens his eyes dreamily to see what he's been sent.
The one and only lonely bug, by now has guessed its fate
As Incy teeters close to him with his drunken ungainly gait.
But which of the many bugs he sees looks good enough to eat
Is it that one there, or that one there, it's really got him beat.
He lunges then in desperation, and totally misses his chance,
Goes spiralling down towards the ground, flying by the seat of his pants
So if you are a spider, living in a cellar with brandy,
Before you try to eat your tea, make sure there's a safety net handy.

Hazel Ratcliffe

FULL CIRCLE

Life goes round in a circle
As season follows season,
Time's span imperceptible,
Birth, death, regeneration.

Hazel Wellings

The Hill Of Life

As you climb the hill,
The hill of life.
You sometimes stumble,
In times of strife.
You often wonder
If you will survive,
Through dark days of sadness,
You need to be revived,
As you climb the hill,
The hill of life,
You search for answers,
You cannot find,
You often wonder,
What is out there?
And it's then you begin
To think about prayer.

Olwena Reed

JENNY'S MORNING POEM

A gentle hum of optimism
Wedged between
The rattle and clink of the milk van
The thud of the paper-boy tabloids
And the postman slapping the post box
With a waste of wood junk mail.

Early morning is the fairest flower
That wilts come afternoon,
Come evening
And the last drops of morning's glitter
Fall prey to thorns in the strangle of the moon.

So waste not this hour
Baked in lonely indecision
Morning is the fairest flower
Draped in garments of silky optimism
Come afternoon reduced to cotton
Come the evening
Not worth a button.

Paul Phelps

THE BLUE TIT

Oh pretty little blue tit, hanging upside down,
Are you an acrobat, or are you a clown?
Maybe you are an artist on the flying trapeze,
For whichever way up you are, you perform your act with ease.

Or, are you a gymnast, full of grace and charm,
Or a noisy little ringmaster, chirping with alarm?
To me, you are a beauty, in your plumage of bright blue,
You fill my heart with gladness, so I ask one thing of you.

'Oh pretty little blue tit, sitting in the tree,
Please come on down and make your home with me.'

Margaret Pawson

PRINCESS FOR A DAY

An off the shoulder wedding dress
Princess for a day
Long veil and tiara
Sequence from a play

A role, but one of many
She'll play throughout her life
A mother and a worker
And a loving wife

Today is something special
An audience is allowed
Who bring gifts for the loving couple
One big happy crowd

The atmosphere is a happy one
With music, food, and drink
When everyone enjoys themselves
Some, too much I think

The night is drawing on now
The crowd leaves, one by one
There, shaking hands and smiling
All have had their fun

The princess will be changing
Playing a new part
Whatever part she's playing
She'll play it from the heart.

B Page

Our Pendle

When I awake each morning
What a splendid sight I see
There's Pendle, like a sentinel
Guarding you and me.

I turn my eyes towards the west
When evening shadows fall,
And I stand in awe and bewilderment
At the beauty of it all.

The sight no millionaire could buy
No President or King
No oil tycoon or foreign prince
Could buy our Pendle Hill.

Whenever I wander overseas
In search of beauty rare,
There's nothing in this great big world
With Pendle to compare
She never fails us night or day
With her majesty and might
Our heritage for all to see
This marvellous, wondrous sight.

Doris Shire

LIFELINE

I was yours, you were mine
Misty dew mornings
Glistening through our yearnings
First rays of sunshine
Laugher and joy
First a girl and then a boy
Happiness abound, so much love to cherish
When or where did it all but perish
Black thunderous cold clouds
Screaming and crying aloud
Dreams lay scattered, trodden on the black Earth, sodden
Hearts cracked and broken
Words never easily spoken
Bled slowly inside as they desperately try to hide
Pain, fear, isolation on one cares to find
Eyes that shine brightly
Yet seek to be blind
River of tears flowing
Faces see but not showing
Leaving it all to ebb gently toward the never-ending tide
As united, they try to be a family inside.

Katherine Quaye

A Dream Just Before Wakening

A mild but sudden intake of breath -
Flames flickering gently from slim, cream candles,
Reflecting in the oak-topped table's polished gleam -
As she slides silently, elegantly, into her seat alongside mine,
Hair in the French style, rolled back neatly, one wisp straying,
To curl alluringly, tantalisingly, just above an eye,
Eyes which gaze frankly, appraisingly,
But with promise of friendship, into mine.
Eschewing protocol, she lifts the bottle, tilts and pours,
We both watch as the fizzing foam subsides
And minute bubbles make their beady way up to the rim,
She lifts her glass and I lift mine,
She smiles, I smile, and in continuing silence
Incline our glasses each toward the other
In mutual toast, then sip.
How has she come, from where and why to me?
I do not care, and if I feel light-headed, well why not?
I'm drinking pink champagne with Barbra Streisand.

Barry Jones

MARCH MOON

The hill strains under tight laced roots
like a Victorian woman's waist
swollen from appreciative eating.

The wind whips blades of grass
flat cap over primrose shoots,
rabbit warrens, crumbling mash
of Earth and stone beneath a solitary tree
where Milly, under a mad March moon,
plays pancakes with a stolen mouse.

Dione Burrow

My Favourite Things

I have a nice collection
Of things I like so much
They are soft and cuddly
And very nice to touch.
I'm talking of my teddies
Of sizes great and small
They come in different colours
To me they're best of all
So when I go car booting
To buy a thing or two
You can bet a teddy bear
Will come back with me too.

Sheila Elkins

HUSH BE QUIET!

Oh look! There's a bird,
Hush, be quiet, not a word!
The bird you see, cannot fly,
Thought to myself, I wonder why?
Realised it had hurt its wing,
My young daughter looked at it and said
'Oh you poor little thing'
Then picked it up and stroked its plume,
Said 'Can I please take it home
To keep it warm and free from harm?'
Suddenly, it leaped from her hand,
It was frightened, you understand.
I thought my girl was going to cry,
As it was caught again, she gave a sigh.
The bird was put in a safe place,
Amongst bracken, bushes and trees,
A smile broke out on my girl's face,
As she voiced her pleas.

B W Jones

CHILDREN ARE LENT TO US, NOT GIVEN

She broke my heart today,
She flew the nest,
She flew away,
She broke my heart today,
She said she wouldn't stay.
I felt so crushed,
I felt so sore.
The moment she stepped through the door,
She broke my heart today,
The moment she flew away,
I look at her in a different light,
She seems to have grown over night.
I remember when she was small,
So pretty, so dainty, now so tall.
I sit and think awhile,
With affection
With a smile.
Of all the fun that we've had,
All I feel now is sad.
I know there were rows,
I know there were tears.
But I really thought
I'd got her here for years and years.
Oh, how she's broken my heart today,
The tiny chick has grown into a beautiful bird
        and flown away.

Sally Hunter

AN AVENUE TO KNOWLEDGE

There is a library to study works of various authors.
What a treasure of books for the benefit of all of us.

Vision and art is waiting there, if you have a quest.
You can find the difference between fiction and fact.

I always try to find some time somehow or other,
To visit this place in search of the truth, however.

Apprehended by the human tragedies in store,
To stimulate my burning desire a little more.

In consistence with the vigilant quality of a man,
Through extensive dimensions of the human brain.

New roses on new horizons, if you want to grow,
This place could help you, if you want to know.

Even though there are top secrets of nature, many more,
A standing challenge for human curiosity to explore.

M Yaqub Mirza

THE DEPARTMENT STORE AFTER SIXTY YEARS

No more ceramic artistry:
Picturesque old cottages,
Graceful birds, lithe animals;
Sailing ships in bottles.

No more tempting kitchenware;
Clean, attractive stationery;
Trays of Christmas baubles,
Or a lovely Christmas Grotto.

No fashions departments;
Restaurant and food store;
Bank and travel agency,
Or large, impressive staircase.

No comfortable feelings
Inside this store, now empty.
It's just a stately building
Full of pleasant memories.

Dora Hawkins

NOISE

The world is such a noisy place
Everything moves at such a pace
Hissing airbrakes, banging doors
Roller-skates on concrete floors

Jumbo jets, high speed trains
Hooting cars on busy lanes
Stereo music, barking dogs
Huge chain saws, sawing logs

Pneumatic drills, a car alarm
So much noise must do us harm
Yes! This noise is bad I fear
What does it do to the human ear?

Mary Shepherd

INTIMATIONS OF HOPE

With echoes of the ancient wisdom whispering faintly from the womb,
the child, who grows in stature daily, plagued by violence,
                                              discord, gloom;
hears no more those mystic voices teaching secrets of its being
given to them at their conception. Soon the eye of truth all seeing,
from the youth no longer caring, fades and dies. It's precious vision
nevermore to be recaptured in this turmoiled indecision.
Understanding not the learning, stunted by an aimless growing,
blinded by the lights of progress, cheated of its birthright knowing.

These secrets then are substituted by their parent's superstition,
where the seeds of hate are sown, germinated through religion.
The youth that was, now seeks for learning from the voice of those
who try to shine a light within this darkness. But their well of life
                                                      stands dry.
Prejudice then feeds the fires which burn within them unabated.
Some believe, through words alone, a road to Heaven can be created.
Yet still the world of inspiration tries to penetrate this night
to shine the way to joys unknown for all to share its glorious light

Then overcome by life's cruel pressures, each appearing in their season,
hour by hour they struggle daily, hearing not the voice of reason
amid the clamour of their striving, forging mighty prison chains.
Too late they find that in their making by the anvils leaping flames,
all their strength is dissipating, the glass near empty of its sand.
Whilst blindly groping in their darkness, grasps the brutal jailer's hand.
Yet like the monkey, hand in vessel, now a prisoner through its greed,
cannot see it can be free, by dropping what it does not need.
So round it runs in little circles, refusing to release its prize,
but when the hunter fast approaches, wishes that it had been wise.

Januarius

QUESTIONS!

Who I am? I do not know,
I see the clouds,
which grow with confidence and elegance.
Am I a cloud?
Am I a human being with knowledge and wisdom,
compassion, a sense of duty to others?
Or am I something which reflects to the distance
and expands to the universe, beyond our own comprehension?
Or I am simply looking for questions, which have no answers!

Dev Dhaliwal

As I Looked Out Of The Window

As I looked out of the window
In the balmy bright moonlight of June
I was surprised to see in the garden
A little pig playing a tune.

He bowed from the waist when he saw me
And proffered his pipe, so polite.
I stared at his breeches, his big brass buttons,
And said 'It's the middle of the night!'

'So what?' he replied, rather coarsely,
Returning the pipe to his mouth.
'The best time to play, if you ask me,
A fact I discovered in youth.'

I pondered this point for a moment,
Reluctant to row with a pig,
Then said with a morsel of malice
'Next you'll be dancing a jig!'

'No problem!' He paused unconcernedly,
Pointing his trotters just so.
'If you'll be so kind as to tell me
Which way you want me to go?'

'To the left, to the right,' I retorted,
'Backwards or forwards all night.
Whatever you do doesn't matter,
A pig on its hind legs ain't right!'

I slammed down the window in chagrin,
Leaving him porcine but frisky,
Fell on the bed, reached for my glass
And another bottle of whiskey.

M Carr

FAREWELL TO STAN

In pre-dawn dark and winter wet
The bleak cold day began.
Etched memory now, I'll not forget
That farewell to our friend Stan.

Early at the quiet church,
All empty save for Stan,
Mind and soul in silence search -
How can one understand?

Brave daughters lead and help support
Their windswept Mother fair.
It hurts to see her so distraught,
- Grief aching beyond compare.

The end of all is in this scene?
- Two hundred sing the closing hymn -
What depth of love must there have been
Such depth of grief to bring.

Red rose of anguish and of love
Laid one by one those three,
Whilst all around scarce move was made
Save to comfort that family.

Douglas Bryan Kennett

The Bluebell Wood

What a lovely scene of pure delight
Displayed before our wondering eyes,
This woodland host of ancient trees
That rise towards the sunlit skies,
And at their feet this canopy,
A wondrous carpet of heavenly blue,
Where masses of bluebells bestrew the ground,
Beguiling us with their perfume and hue.

We walk along the winding paths,
Each bend revealing among the trees
More masses of bluebells in all their glory,
Our hearts to gladden, our eyes to please;
There are also scattered groups of wild flowers
Each with its own colour shade;
The whole picture leads us on to declare
That this is indeed a fairy glade.

As we feast upon this lovely scene
Another pleasure beguiles the ear,
Amongst the freshly leafing trees
We hear birds singing, sweet and clear;
Then as we reach the edge of the wood
We suddenly discover a badger sett,
Which really helps to make our day,
A day that we will not forget.

Now it's time to wend our homeward way
With visions of beauty still in our eyes,
The wonder of this lovely place
Never ceases to make our spirits rise,
And we give thanks for this wondrous world,
This world of hills and valleys and seas,
Of flowers and grasslands and silver lakes,
And the glory of the graceful trees!

Bernard Laughton

MOONLIGHT

Across the blackened sky at night
Stares the moon in apparel bright,
Above the roof line there in view
This luminary of celestial hue.

Its guiding light strikes everywhere
From dusty pane to creaking stair
And likewise in this hour of gloom
Bleached beams are sent across my room
For there upon a wall I see
Reflected shadows of a shivering tree.

Then as the hours of night give way to dawn
Increasing brightness heralds the morn
So fading moon's cold light is done
As the new day brings the warmth of sun.

Alistair L Lawrence

THOUGHTS IN DROUGHT

Let it rain, rain, rain,
Starting softly, gaining volume,
Trickling down the window pane
Overflowing pools and puddles
Blotting out the driver's vision
Soaking the pedestrian's clothes
Falling from a leaden sky
Seeping in through doors and windows
Spreading dampness all around.

Let the dogs all scurry, dripping,
Back from walks across the moor
And the cows be pressed together
In a corner of the field
Let the trees all stand bedraggled
Shedding pleasurable tears
Clapping their symbolic hands
Let the grass stand up and cheer
For the coming of the rain.
Let the children laugh and giggle
Taking off their soaking clothes
As they watch the lovely rain.

When the sun comes out again
It will dazzle, it will sparkle.
It will shine with brilliant rays
Seven times its normal brightness
Like the light of seven days
After the refreshing rain.

Christina Hanson

ESTUARY

Every time dark clouds choke the sun
I do not seek shelter, I wait for the rain.
You taught me there is warmth in love,
I learned that cold can build up trust.

Every time I feel like I am falling,
I beat my wings. You pull myself up,
After soaring to my endless dreams,
You showed me springs behind mountains.

Every time I doubt for tomorrow,
I love you even more. You are my hope.
Because I know you will be there too,
I can stand where the river meets the sea.

Zardee Emmanuel Garagan

FOOTBALL

I've nothing against football
No! I've nothing against it at all
It's just when I switch on my tele
All I get is 'Football! Football! Football!'
So what can I do to change things
As it's beginning to get such a bore?
Shall I get rid of my tele . . .
Oh no, no, no!
I'll just put up with it all.

D Stripling

THE ANGELUS

At the end of a long day
I sit out in the glen
All is quiet and tranquil
As I watch the evening in.

A frog sits on a lily pad
In waters so deep
Out pops his tongue and grabs a fly
A meal for him to eat.

All is quiet around me,
As the evening star appears
The Angelus is sounding
From a distant church.

People into the church they wander
A last prayer to make
They cross themselves with Holy water
And sweet praises they make.

Neilea Hames

Dogs

Dogs are funny they play with everyone,
They rush about everywhere but they don't care.
Dogs are big and small and sometimes even tall,
They stop and stare because they like to scare.

Nicole Jenkins (8)

WEATHERS

This is the weather the winter bears like,
And so do I.
When freezing ice turns into spikes,
And hooting owls fly.
And children have a snowball fight,
And mums and dads shout with all their might.
Santa Claus puts his suit on tight,
And in the dark nights children shiver with fright.
And so do I.

Siobhan Jenkins (10)

ANCHOR BOOKS
SUBMISSIONS INVITED
SOMETHING FOR EVERYONE

ANCHOR BOOKS GEN - Any subject, light-hearted clean fun, nothing unprintable please.

THE OPPOSITE SEX - Have your say on the opposite gender. Do they drive you mad or can we co-exist in harmony?

THE NATURAL WORLD - Are we destroying the world around us? What should we do to preserve the beauty and the future of our planet - you decide!

All poems no longer than 30 lines.
Always welcome! No fee!
Plus cash prizes to be won!

Mark your envelope (eg *The Natural World*)
And send to:
Anchor Books
Remus House, Coltsfoot Drive
Peterborough, PE2 9JX

**OVER £10,000 IN POETRY PRIZES
TO BE WON!**

Send an SAE for details on our New Year 2002 competition!